E. Leutze. Phillibrown

Seated by gallant Hotspur's side,
His Katherine was a happy bride
A Thousand years ago.

Seated by gallant Hotspur's side,
His Katherine was a happy bride
A Thousand years ago.

Alnwick Castle

POEMS

By

FITZ-GREENE HALLECK.

With dancing hair and laughing eyes,
That seem to mock me as it flies.

Magdalen

NEW YORK,
D. APPLETON, & Cº 200 BROADWAY.

THE

POETICAL WORKS

OF

FITZ-GREENE HALLECK.

NOW FIRST COLLECTED.

ILLUSTRATED WITH STEEL ENGRAVINGS,

From Drawings by American Artists.

SECOND EDITION.

NEW YORK:
D. APPLETON & COMPANY, 200 BROADWAY.
PHILADELPHIA:
GEO. S. APPLETON, 148 CHESNUT STREET.
M DCCC XLVIII.

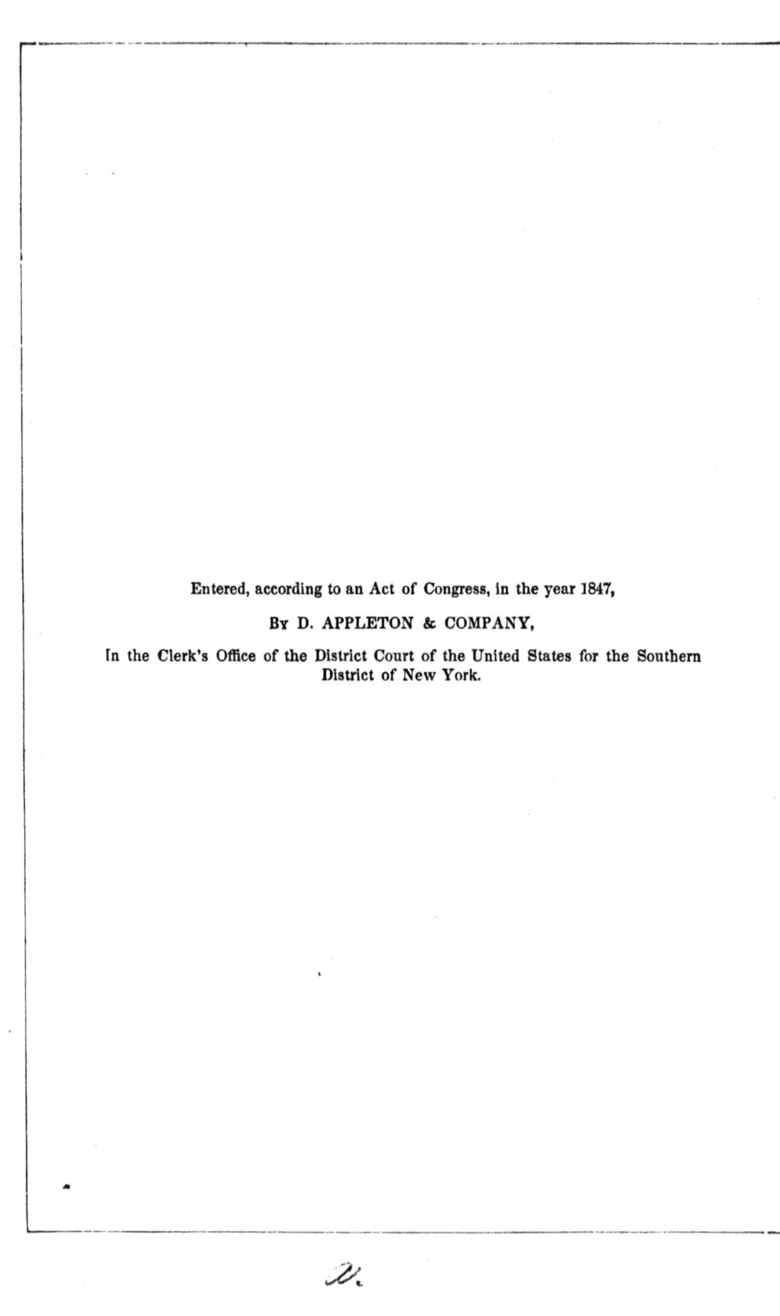

CONTENTS.

CONTENTS.

EPISTLES, ETC.

LIST OF THE ILLUSTRATIONS.

THE MOTHER.

BY D. HUNTINGTON.

"Come to the mother's, when she feels,
For the first time, her first-born's breath."

MARCO BOZZARIS, p. 22.

LANDSCAPE.

PAINTED BY A. B. DURAND.

"My own green forest-land."

BURNS, p. 35.

THE HOUSE TO LET.

PAINTED BY F. W. EDMONDS.

"The song of knocker and of bell was over;
Upon the steps two chimney sweeps reposed;
And on the door my dazzled eyebeam met
These cabalistic words—'this house to let.'"

FANNY, p. 202.

Yours truly,
Fitz-Greene Halleck

POEMS.

ALNWICK CASTLE.[1]

Home of the Percy's high-born race,
  Home of their beautiful and brave,
Alike their birth and burial place,
  Their cradle and their grave!
Still sternly o'er the castle gate
Their house's Lion stands in state,
  As in his proud departed hours;
And warriors frown in stone on high,
And feudal banners "flout the sky"
  Above his princely towers.

A gentle hill its side inclines,
  Lovely in England's fadeless green,

To meet the quiet stream which winds
  Through this romantic scene
As silently and sweetly still,
As when, at evening, on that hill,
  While summer's wind blew soft and low,
Seated by gallant Hotspur's side,
His Katharine was a happy bride,
  A thousand years ago.

Gaze on the Abbey's ruined pile:
  Does not the succoring ivy, keeping
Her watch around it, seem to smile,
  As o'er a loved one sleeping?
One solitary turret gray
  Still tells, in melancholy glory,
The legend of the Cheviot day,
  The Percy's proudest border story.
That day its roof was triumph's arch;
  Then rang, from aisle to pictured dome,

The light step of the soldier's march,
  The music of the trump and drum;
And babe, and sire, the old, the young,
And the monk's hymn, and minstrel's song,
And woman's pure kiss, sweet and long,
  Welcomed her warrior home.

Wild roses by the Abbey towers
  Are gay in their young bud and bloom:
They were born of a race of funeral flowers
That garlanded, in long-gone hours,
  A Templar's knightly tomb.
He died, the sword in his mailed hand,
On the holiest spot of the Blessed Land,
  Where the Cross was damped with his dying
      breath,
When blood ran free as festal wine,
And the sainted air of Palestine
  Was thick with the darts of death.

Wise with the lore of centuries,
What tales, if there be "tongues in trees,"
Those giant oaks could tell,
Of beings born and buried here;
Tales of the peasant and the peer,
Tales of the bridal and the bier,
The welcome and farewell,
Since on their boughs the startled bird
First, in her twilight slumbers, heard
The Norman's curfew-bell.

I wandered through the lofty halls
Trod by the Percys of old fame,
And traced upon the chapel walls
Each high, heroic name,
From him[2] who once his standard set
Where now, o'er mosque and minaret,
Glitter the Sultan's crescent moons;
To him who, when a younger son,[3]

Huntington | Greatbach

What Tales if there be "tongues in trees,"
Those giant oaks could tell,
Of beings born and buried here.

Alnwick Castle

Fought for King George at Lexington,
  A major of dragoons.

*   *   *   *

That last half stanza—it has dashed
  From my warm lip the sparkling cup;
The light that o'er my eyebeam flashed,
  The power that bore my spirit up
Above this bank-note world—is gone;
And Alnwick's but a market town,
And this, alas! its market day,
And beasts and borderers throng the way;
Oxen and bleating lambs in lots,
Northumbrian boors and plaided Scots,
  Men in the coal and cattle line;
From Teviot's bard and hero land,
From royal Berwick's[4] beach of sand,
From Wooller, Morpeth, Hexham, and
  Newcastle-upon-Tyne.

These are not the romantic times
So beautiful in Spenser's rhymes,
  So dazzling to the dreaming boy:
Ours are the days of fact, not fable,
Of knights, but not of the Round Table,
  Of Bailie Jarvie, not Rob Roy:
'Tis what "our president," Monroe,
  Has called "the era of good feeling:"
The Highlander, the bitterest foe
To modern laws, has felt their blow,
Consented to be taxed, and vote,
And put on pantaloons and coat,
  And leave off cattle-stealing:
Lord Stafford mines for coal and salt,
The Duke of Norfolk deals in malt,
  The Douglass in red herrings;
And noble name and cultured land,
Palace, and park, and vassal band,
Are powerless to the notes of hand
  Of Rothschild or the Barings.

The age of bargaining, said Burke,
Has come: to-day the turbaned Turk
(Sleep, Richard of the lion heart!
Sleep on, nor from your cerements start),
  Is England's friend and fast ally;
The Moslem tramples on the Greek,
  And on the Cross and altar stone,
  And Christendom looks tamely on,
And hears the Christian maiden shriek,
  And sees the Christian father die;
And not a sabre blow is given
For Greece and fame, for faith and heaven,
  By Europe's craven chivalry.

You'll ask if yet the Percy lives
  In the armed pomp of feudal state?
The present representatives
  Of Hotspur and his "gentle Kate,"
Are some half-dozen serving men,

In the drab coat of William Penn;
  A chambermaid, whose lip and eye,
And cheek, and brown hair, bright and curling,
  Spoke nature's aristocracy;
And one, half groom, half seneschal,
Who bowed me through court, bower, and hall,
From donjon-keep to turret wall,
For ten-and-sixpence sterling.

MARCO BOZZARIS.[5]

At midnight, in his guarded tent,
The Turk was dreaming of the hour
When Greece, her knee in suppliance bent,
Should tremble at his power:
In dreams, through camp and court, he bore
The trophies of a conqueror;
In dreams his song of triumph heard;
Then wore his monarch's signet ring:
Then pressed that monarch's throne—a king;
As wild his thoughts, and gay of wing,
As Eden's garden bird.

At midnight, in the forest shades,
  Bozzaris ranged his Suliote band,
True as the steel of their tried blades,
  Heroes in heart and hand.
There had the Persian's thousands stood,
There had the glad earth drunk their blood
  On old Platæa's day;
And now there breathed that haunted air
The sons of sires who conquered there,
With arm to strike, and soul to dare,
  As quick, as far as they.

An hour passed on—the Turk awoke;
  That bright dream was his last;
He woke—to hear his sentries shriek,
"To arms! they come! the Greek! the Greek!"
He woke—to die midst flame, and smoke,
And shout, and groan, and sabre stroke,
  And death shots falling thick and fast

As lightnings from the mountain cloud;
And heard, with voice as trumpet loud,
  Bozzaris cheer his band:
"Strike—till the last armed foe expires;
Strike—for your altars and your fires;
Strike—for the green graves of your sires;
  God—and your native land!"

They fought—like brave men, long and well;
  They piled that ground with Moslem slain,
They conquered—but Bozzaris fell,
  Bleeding at every vein.
His few surviving comrades saw
His smile when rang their proud hurrah,
  And the red field was won;
Then saw in death his eyelids close
Calmly, as to a night's repose,
  Like flowers at set of sun.

Come to the bridal chamber, Death!
  Come to the mother's, when she feels,
For the first time, her first-born's breath;
  Come when the blessed seals
That close the pestilence are broke,
And crowded cities wail its stroke;
Come in consumption's ghastly form,
The earthquake shock, the ocean storm;
Come when the heart beats high and warm,
  With banquet song, and dance, and wine;
And thou art terrible—the tear,
The groan, the knell, the pall, the bier;
And all we know, or dream, or fear
  Of agony, are thine.

But to the hero, when his sword
  Has won the battle for the free,
Thy voice sounds like a prophet's word;
And in its hollow tones are heard

Huntington Phillibrown

Come to the mothers, when she feels
For the first time, her first born's breath.

The thanks of millions yet to be.
Come, when his task of fame is wrought—
Come, with her laurel-leaf, blood-bought—
Come in her crowning hour—and then
Thy sunken eye's unearthly light
To him is welcome as the sight
Of sky and stars to prisoned men:
Thy grasp is welcome as the hand
Of brother in a foreign land;
Thy summons welcome as the cry
That told the Indian isles were nigh
To the world-seeking Genoese,
When the land wind, from woods of palm,
And orange groves, and fields of balm,
Blew o'er the Haytian seas.

Bozzaris! with the storied brave
Greece nurtured in her glory's time,
Rest thee—there is no prouder grave,

Even in her own proud clime.
She wore no funeral weeds for thee,
Nor bade the dark hearse wave its plume,
Like torn branch from death's leafless tree
In sorrow's pomp and pageantry,
The heartless luxury of the tomb:
But she remembers thee as one
Long loved, and for a season gone;
For thee her poet's lyre is wreathed,
Her marble wrought, her music breathed;
For thee she rings the birthday bells;
Of thee her babes' first lisping tells;
For thine her evening prayer is said
At palace couch and cottage bed;
Her soldier, closing with the foe,
Gives for thy sake a deadlier blow;
His plighted maiden, when she fears
For him, the joy of her young years,
Thinks of thy fate, and checks her tears:
And she, the mother of thy boys,

Though in her eye and faded cheek
Is read the grief she will not speak,
  The memory of her buried joys,
And even she who gave thee birth,
Will, by their pilgrim-circled hearth,
  Talk of thy doom without a sigh:
For thou art Freedom's now, and Fame's;
One of the few, the immortal names,
  That were not born to die.

BURNS.

TO A ROSE, BROUGHT FROM NEAR ALLOWAY KIRK, IN AYRSHIRE, IN THE AUTUMN OF 1822.

Wild Rose of Alloway! my thanks:
  Thou 'mindst me of that autumn noon
When first we met upon "the banks
  And braes o' bonny Doon."

Like thine, beneath the thorn-tree's bough,
  My sunny hour was glad and brief,
We've crossed the winter sea, and thou
  Art withered—flower and leaf.

And will not thy death-doom be mine—
  The doom of all things wrought of clay—
And withered my life's leaf like thine,
  Wild rose of Alloway?

Not so his memory, for whose sake
  My bosom bore thee far and long,
His—who a humbler flower could make
  Immortal as his song.

The memory of Burns—a name
  That calls, when brimmed her festal cup,
A nation's glory and her shame,
  In silent sadness up.

A nation's glory—be the rest
  Forgot—she 's canonized his mind;
And it is joy to speak the best
  We may of human kind.

I've stood beside the cottage bed
Where the Bard-peasant first drew breath;
A straw-thatched roof above his head,
A straw-wrought couch beneath.

And I have stood beside the pile,
His monument—that tells to Heaven
The homage of earth's proudest isle
To that Bard-peasant given!

Bid thy thoughts hover o'er that spot,
Boy-Minstrel, in thy dreaming hour;
And know, however low his lot,
A Poet's pride and power.

The pride that lifted Burns from earth,
The power that gave a child of song
Ascendency o'er rank and birth,
The rich, the brave, the strong;

And if despondency weigh down
  Thy spirit's fluttering pinions then,
Despair—thy name is written on
  The roll of common men.

There have been loftier themes than his,
  And longer scrolls, and louder lyres,
And lays lit up with Poesy's
  Purer and holier fires:

Yet read the names that know not death;
  Few nobler ones than Burns are there;
And few have won a greener wreath
  Than that which binds his hair.

His is that language of the heart,
  In which the answering heart would speak,
Thought, word, that bids the warm tear start,
  Or the smile light the cheek;

And his that music, to whose tone
  The common pulse of man keeps time,
In cot or castle's mirth or moan,
  In cold or sunny clime.

And who hath heard his song, nor knelt
  Before its spell with willing knee,
And listened, and believed, and felt
  The Poet's mastery

O'er the mind's sea, in calm and storm,
  O'er the heart's sunshine and its showers,
O'er Passion's moments, bright and warm,
  O'er Reason's dark, cold hours;

On fields where brave men "die or do,"
  In halls where rings the banquet's mirth,
Where mourners weep, where lovers woo,
  From throne to cottage hearth?

What sweet tears dim the eyes unshed,
  What wild vows falter on the tongue,
When "Scots wha hae wi' Wallace bled,"
  Or "Auld Lang Syne" is sung!

Pure hopes, that lift the soul above,
  Come with his Cotter's hymn of praise,
And dreams of youth, and truth, and love,
  With "Logan's" banks and braes.

And when he breathes his master-lay
  Of Alloway's witch-haunted wall,
All passions in our frames of clay
  Come thronging at his call.

Imagination's world of air,
  And our own world, its gloom and glee,
Wit, pathos, poetry, are there,
  And death's sublimity.

And Burns—though brief the race he ran,
  Though rough and dark the path he trod,
Lived—died—in form and soul a Man,
  The image of his God.

Through care, and pain, and want, and wo,
  With wounds that only death could heal,
Tortures—the poor alone can know,
  The proud alone can feel;

He kept his honesty and truth,
  His independent tongue and pen,
And moved, in manhood as in youth,
  Pride of his fellow men.

Strong sense, deep feeling, passions strong,
  A hate of tyrant and of knave,
A love of right, a scorn of wrong,
  Of coward and of slave;

A kind, true heart, a spirit high,
  That could not fear and would not bow,
Were written in his manly eye
  And on his manly brow.

Praise to the bard! his words are driven,
  Like flower-seeds by the far winds sown,
Where'er, beneath the sky of heaven,
  The birds of fame have flown.

Praise to the man! a nation stood
  Beside his coffin with wet eyes,
Her brave, her beautiful, her good,
  As when a loved one dies.

And still, as on his funeral day,
  Men stand his cold earth-couch around,
With the mute homage that we pay
  To consecrated ground.

And consecrated ground it is,
The last, the hallowed home of one
Who lives upon all memories,
Though with the buried gone.

Such graves as his are pilgrim-shrines,
Shrines to no code or creed confined—
The Delphian vales, the Palestines,
The Meccas of the mind.

Sages, with wisdom's garland wreathed,
Crowned kings, and mitred priests of power,
And warriors with their bright swords sheathed,
The mightiest of the hour;

And lowlier names, whose humble home
Is lit by Fortune's dimmer star,
Are there—o'er wave and mountain come,
From countries near and far;

A.B.Durand. P.N.A.D. James Smillie.

"MY OWN GREEN FOREST LAND."

New-York D. Appleton & Co.

Pilgrims whose wandering feet have pressed
  The Switzer's snow, the Arab's sand,
Or trod the piled leaves of the West,
  My own green forest-land.

All ask the cottage of his birth,
  Gaze on the scenes he loved and sung,
And gather feelings not of earth
  His fields and streams among.

They linger by the Doon's low trees,
  And pastoral Nith, and wooded Ayr,
And round thy sepulchres, Dumfries!
  The poet's tomb is there.

But what to them the sculptor's art,
  His funeral columns, wreaths, and urns?
Wear they not graven on the heart
  The name of Robert Burns?

WYOMING.[6]

"Dites si la Nature n'a pas fait ce beau pays pour une Julie, pour une Claire, et pour un St. Preux, mais ne les y cherchez pas."—Rousseau.

I.

Thou com'st, in beauty, on my gaze at last,
"On Susquehanna's side, fair Wyoming!"
Image of many a dream, in hours long past,
When life was in its bud and blossoming,
And waters, gushing from the fountain spring
Of pure enthusiast thought, dimmed my young eyes,
As by the poet borne, on unseen wing,
I breathed, in fancy, 'neath thy cloudless skies,
The summer's air, and heard her echoed harmonies.

II.

I then but dreamed: thou art before me now,
In life, a vision of the brain no more.
I've stood upon the wooded mountain's brow,
That beetles high thy lovely valley o'er;
And now, where winds thy river's greenest shore,
Within a bower of sycamores am laid;
And winds, as soft and sweet as ever bore
The fragrance of wild flowers through sun and shade,
Are singing in the trees, whose low boughs press my head.

III.

Nature hath made thee lovelier than the power
Even of Campbell's pen hath pictured: he
Had woven, had he gazed one sunny hour
Upon thy smiling vale, its scenery
With more of truth, and made each rock and tree
Known like old friends, and greeted from afar:
And there are tales of sad reality,

In the dark legends of thy border war,
With woes of deeper tint than his own Gertrude's are.

IV.

But where are they, the beings of the mind,
The bard's creations, moulded not of clay,
Hearts to strange bliss and suffering assigned—
Young Gertrude, Albert, Waldegrave—where are they?
We need not ask. The people of to-day
Appear good, honest, quiet men enough,
And hospitable too—for ready pay;
With manners like their roads, a little rough,
And hands whose grasp is warm and welcoming, though tough.

V.

Judge Hallenbach, who keeps the toll-bridge gate,
And the town records, is the Albert now

Of Wyoming: like him, in church and state,
Her Doric column; and upon his brow
The thin hairs, white with seventy winters' snow,
Look patriarchal. Waldegrave 'twere in vain
To point out here, unless in yon scare-crow,
That stands full-uniformed upon the plain,
To frighten flocks of crows and blackbirds from the grain.

VI.

For he would look particularly droll
In his "Iberian boot" and "Spanish plume,"
And be the wonder of each Christian soul
As of the birds that scare-crow and his broom.
But Gertrude, in her loveliness and bloom,
Hath many a model here; for woman's eye,
In court or cottage, wheresoe'er her home,
Hath a heart-spell too holy and too high
To be o'erpraised even by her worshipper—Poesy.

VII.

There's one in the next field—of sweet sixteen—
Singing and summoning thoughts of beauty born
In heaven—with her jacket of light green,
" Love-darting eyes, and tresses like the morn,"
Without a shoe or stocking—hoeing corn.
Whether, like Gertrude, she oft wanders there,
With Shakspeare's volume in her bosom borne,
I think is doubtful. Of the poet-player
The maiden knows no more than Cobbett or Voltaire.

VIII.

There is a woman, widowed, gray, and old,
Who tells you where the foot of Battle stepped
Upon their day of massacre. She told
Its tale, and pointed to the spot, and wept,
Whereon her father and five brothers slept
Shroudless, the bright-dreamed slumbers of the brave,
When all the land a funeral mourning kept.

And there, wild laurels planted on the grave
By Nature's hand, in air their pale red blossoms wave.

IX.

And on the margin of yon orchard hill
Are marks where timeworn battlements have been,
And in the tall grass traces linger still
Of "arrowy frieze and wedged ravelin."
Five hundred of her brave that valley green
Trod on the morn in soldier-spirit gay;
But twenty lived to tell the noonday scene—
And where are now the twenty? Passed away.
Has Death no triumph-hours, save on the battle-day?

ON THE DEATH OF

JOSEPH RODMAN DRAKE,

OF NEW-YORK, SEPT., 1820.

"The good die first,
And they, whose hearts are dry as summer dust,
Burn to the socket."

WORDSWORTH.

GREEN be the turf above thee,
  Friend of my better days!
None knew thee but to love thee,
  Nor named thee but to praise.

Tears fell, when thou wert dying,
  From eyes unused to weep,
And long where thou art lying,
  Will tears the cold turf steep.

When hearts, whose truth was proven,
  Like thine, are laid in earth,
There should a wreath be woven
  To tell the world their worth;

And I, who woke each morrow
  To clasp thy hand in mine,
Who shared thy joy and sorrow,
  Whose weal and wo were thine:

It should be mine to braid it
  Around thy faded brow,
But I've in vain essayed it,
  And feel I cannot now.

While memory bids me weep thee,
  Nor thoughts nor words are free,
The grief is fixed too deeply
  That mourns a man like thee.

TWILIGHT.

There is an evening twilight of the heart,
When its wild passion-waves are lulled to rest,
And the eye sees life's fairy scenes depart,
As fades the day-beam in the rosy west.
'Tis with a nameless feeling of regret
We gaze upon them as they melt away,
And fondly would we bid them linger yet,
But Hope is round us with her angel lay,
Hailing afar some happier moonlight hour;
Dear are her whispers still, though lost their early power.

In youth the cheek was crimsoned with her glow;
  Her smile was loveliest then; her matin song
Was heaven's own music, and the note of wo
  Was all unheard her sunny bowers among.
Life's little world of bliss was newly born;
  We knew not, cared not, it was born to die,
Flushed with the cool breeze and the dews of morn,
  With dancing heart we gazed on the pure sky,
And mocked the passing clouds that dimmed its blue,
Like our own sorrows then—as fleeting and as few.

And manhood felt her sway too—on the eye,
  Half realized, her early dreams burst bright,
Her promised bower of happiness seemed nigh,
  Its days of joy, its vigils of delight;
And though at times might lower the thunder-storm,
  And the red lightnings threaten, still the air
Was balmy with her breath, and her loved form,
  The rainbow of the heart, was hovering there.

'Tis in life's noontide she is nearest seen,
Her wreath the summer flower, her robe of summer
green.

But though less dazzling in her twilight dress,
There's more of heaven's pure beam about her now;
That angel-smile of tranquil loveliness,
Which the heart worships, glowing on her brow;
That smile shall brighten the dim evening star
That points our destined tomb, nor e'er depart
Till the faint light of life is fled afar,
And hushed the last deep beating of the heart;
The meteor-bearer of our parting breath,
A moonbeam in the midnight cloud of death.

PSALM CXXXVII.

"By the rivers of Babylon."

We sat us down and wept,
Where Babel's waters slept,
And we thought of home and Zion as a long-gone, happy dream;
We hung our harps in air
On the willow boughs, which there,
Gloomy as round a sepulchre, were drooping o'er the stream.

The foes, whose chain we wore,
Were with us on that shore,
Exulting in our tears that told the bitterness of wo.
"Sing us," they cried aloud,
"Ye, once so high and proud,
The songs ye sang in Zion ere we laid her glory low."

And shall the harp of heaven
To Judah's monarch given
Be touched by captive fingers, or grace a fettered hand?
No! sooner be my tongue
Mute, powerless, and unstrung,
Than its words of holy music make glad a stranger land.

May this right hand, whose skill
Can wake the harp at will,
And bid the listener's joys or griefs in light or darkness come,

Forget its godlike power,
If for one brief, dark hour,
My heart forgets Jerusalem, fallen city of my home!

Daughter of Babylon!
Blessed be that chosen one,
Whom God shall send to smite thee when there is none to save;
He from the mother's breast,
Shall pluck the babe at rest,
And lay it in the sleep of death beside its father's grave.

TO * * * *.

THE world is bright before thee,
  Its summer flowers are thine,
Its calm blue sky is o'er thee,
  Thy bosom Pleasure's shrine;
And thine the sunbeam given
  To Nature's morning hour,
Pure, warm, as when from heaven
  It burst on Eden's bower.

There is a song of sorrow,
  The death-dirge of the gay,
That tells, ere dawn of morrow,
  These charms may melt away,

That sun's bright beam be shaded,
  That sky be blue no more,
The summer flowers be faded,
  And youth's warm promise o'er.

Believe it not—though lonely
  Thy evening home may be;
Though Beauty's bark can only
  Float on a summer sea;
Though Time thy bloom is stealing,
  There's still beyond his art
The wild-flower wreath of feeling,
  The sunbeam of the heart.

THE FIELD OF THE GROUNDED ARMS,

SARATOGA.

STRANGERS! your eyes are on that valley fixed
Intently, as we gaze on vacancy,
　　When the mind's wings o'erspread
　　The spirit-world of dreams.

True, 'tis a scene of loveliness—the bright
Green dwelling of the summer's first-born Hours,
　　Whose wakened leaf and bud
　　Are welcoming the morn.

And morn returns the welcome, sun and cloud
Smile on the green earth from their home in heaven,
    Even as a mother smiles
    Above her cradled boy,

And wreath their light and shade o'er plain and mountain,
O'er sleepless seas of grass whose waves are flowers,
    The river's golden shores,
    The forests of dark pines.

The song of the wild bird is on the wind,
The hum of the wild bee, the music wild
    Of waves upon the bank,
    Of leaves upon the bough.

But all is song and beauty in the land,
Beneath her skies of June; then journey on,
    A thousand scenes like this
    Will greet you ere the eve.

Ye linger yet—ye see not, hear not now
The sunny smile, the music of to-day,
    Your thoughts are wandering up,
    Far up the stream of time;

And boyhood's lore and fireside listened tales
Are rushing on your memories, as ye breathe
    That valley's storied name,
    Field of the grounded arms.

Strangers no more, a kindred "pride of place,"
Pride in the gift of country and of name,
    Speaks in your eye and step—
    Ye tread your native land.

And your high thoughts are on her glory's day,
The solemn sabbath of the week of battle,
    Whose tempests bowed to earth
    Her foeman's banner here.

The forest leaves lay scattered cold and dead,
Upon the withered grass that autumn morn,
    When, with as withered hearts
    And hopes as dead and cold,

A gallant army formed their last array
Upon that field, in silence and deep gloom,
    And at their conqueror's feet
    Laid their war-weapons down.

Sullen and stern, disarmed but not dishonored;
Brave men, but brave in vain, they yielded there:
    The soldier's trial task
    Is not alone "to die."

Honor to chivalry! the conqueror's breath
Stains not the ermine of his foeman's fame,
    Nor mocks his captive's doom—
    The bitterest cup of war.

But be that bitterest cup the doom of all
Whose swords are lightning flashes in the cloud
    Of the Invader's wrath,
    Threatening a gallant land.

His armies' trumpet-tones wake not alone
Her slumbering echoes; from a thousand hills
    Her answering voices shout,
    And her bells ring to arms!

Then danger hovers o'er the Invader's march,
On raven wings, hushing the song of fame,
    And glory's hues of beauty
    Fade from the cheek of death.

A foe is heard in every rustling leaf,
A fortress seen in every rock and tree,
    The eagle eye of art
    Is dim and powerless then,

And war becomes a people's joy, the drum
Man's merriest music, and the field of death
    His couch of happy dreams,
    After life's harvest home.

He battles heart and arm, his own blue sky
Above him, and his own green land around,
    Land of his father's grave,
    His blessing and his prayers,

Land where he learned to lisp a mother's name,
The first beloved in life, the last forgot,
    Land of his frolic youth,
    Land of his bridal eve,

Land of his children—vain your columned strength,
Invaders! vain your battles' steel and fire!
    Choose ye the morrow's doom—
    A prison or a grave.

And such were Saratoga's victors—such
The Yeomen-Brave, whose deeds and death have given
  A glory to her skies,
  A music to her name.

In honorable life her fields they trod,
In honorable death they sleep below;
  Their sons' proud feelings here
  Their noblest monuments.

RED JACKET.

A CHIEF OF THE INDIAN TRIBES, THE TUSCARORAS.

ON LOOKING AT HIS PORTRAIT BY WEIR.

COOPER, whose name is with his country's woven,
First in her files, her PIONEER of mind—
A wanderer now in other climes, has proven
His love for the young land he left behind;[7]

And throned her in the senate-hall of nations,
Robed like the deluge rainbow, heaven-wrought;
Magnificent as his own mind's creations,
And beautiful as its green world of thought;

And faithful to the Act of Congress, quoted
As law authority, it passed nem. con.:
He writes that we are, as ourselves have voted,
The most enlightened people ever known.

That all our week is happy as a Sunday
In Paris, full of song, and dance, and laugh;
And that, from Orleans to the Bay of Fundy,
There's not a bailiff or an epitaph.

And furthermore—in fifty years, or sooner,
We shall export our poetry and wine;
And our brave fleet, eight frigates and a schooner,
Will sweep the seas from Zembla to the Line.

If he were with me, King of Tuscarora!
Gazing, as I, upon thy portrait now,
In all its medalled, fringed, and beaded glory,
Its eye's dark beauty, and its thoughtful brow—

Its brow, half martial and half diplomatic,
Its eye, upsoaring like an eagle's wings;
Well might he boast that we, the Democratic,
Outrival Europe, even in our Kings!

For thou wast monarch born. Tradition's pages
Tell not the planting of thy parent tree,
But that the forest tribes have bent for ages
To thee, and to thy sires, the subject knee.

Thy name is princely—if no poet's magic
Could make RED JACKET grace an English rhyme,
Though some one with a genius for the tragic
Hath introduced it in a pantomime,

Yet it is music in the language spoken
Of thine own land; and on her herald roll;
As bravely fought for, and as proud a token
As Cœur de Lion's of a warrior's soul.

Thy garb—though Austria's bosom-star would frighten
  That medal pale, as diamonds the dark mine,
And George the Fourth wore, at his court at Brighton,
  A more becoming evening dress than thine;

Yet 'tis a brave one, scorning wind and weather,
  And fitted for thy couch, on field and flood,
As Rob Roy's tartan for the Highland heather,
  Or forest green for England's Robin Hood.

Is strength a monarch's merit, like a whaler's?
  Thou art as tall, as sinewy, and as strong
As earth's first kings—the Argo's gallant sailors,
  Heroes in history, and gods in song.

Is beauty?—Thine has with thy youth departed;
  But the love-legends of thy manhood's years,
And she who perished, young and broken-hearted,
  Are—but I rhyme for smiles and not for tears.

Is eloquence?—Her spell is thine that reaches
  The heart, and makes the wisest head its sport;
And there's one rare, strange virtue in thy speeches,
  The secret of their mastery—they are short.

The monarch mind, the mystery of commanding,
  The birth-hour gift, the art Napoleon,
Of winning, fettering, moulding, wielding, banding
  The hearts of millions till they move as one;

Thou hast it. At thy bidding men have crowded
  The road to death as to a festival;
And minstrels, at their sepulchres, have shrouded
  With banner-folds of glory the dark pall.

Who will believe? Not I—for in deceiving
  Lies the dear charm of life's delightful dream;
I cannot spare the luxury of believing
  That all things beautiful are what they seem;

Who will believe that, with a smile whose blessing
Would, like the Patriarch's, sooth a dying hour,
With voice as low, as gentle, and caressing,
As e'er won maiden's lip in moonlit bower;

With look, like patient Job's, eschewing evil;
With motions graceful as a bird's in air;
Thou art, in sober truth, the veriest devil
That e'er clenched fingers in a captive's hair!

That in thy breast there springs a poison fountain,
Deadlier than that where bathes the Upas-tree;
And in thy wrath, a nursing cat-o'-mountain
Is calm as her babe's sleep compared with thee!

And underneath that face, like summer ocean's,
Its lip as moveless, and its cheek as clear,
Slumbers a whirlwind of the heart's emotions,
Love, hatred, pride, hope, sorrow—all save fear.

Love—for thy land, as if she were thy daughter,
  Her pipe in peace, her tomahawk in wars;
Hatred—of missionaries and cold water;
  Pride—in thy rifle-trophies and thy scars;

Hope—that thy wrongs may be, by the Great Spirit,
  Remembered and revenged when thou art gone;
Sorrow—that none are left thee to inherit
  Thy name, thy fame, thy passions, and thy throne!

LOVE.

. . . . The imperial votress passed on
In maiden meditation, fancy free.
Midsummer Night's Dream

Shall I never see a bachelor of threescore again?
BENEDICT, *in Much Ado about Nothing*

I.

WHEN the tree of LOVE is budding first,
Ere yet its leaves are green,
Ere yet, by shower and sunbeam nursed
Its infant life has been;
The wild bee's slightest touch might wring
The buds from off the tree,
As the gentle dip of the swallow's wing
Breaks the bubbles on the sea.

II.

But when its open leaves have found
  A home in the free air,
Pluck them, and there remains a wound
  That ever rankles there.
The blight of hope and happiness
  Is felt when fond ones part,
And the bitter tear that follows is
  The life-blood of the heart.

III.

When the flame of love is kindled first,
  'Tis the fire-fly's light at even,
'Tis dim as the wandering stars that burst
  In the blue of the summer heaven.
A breath can bid it burn no more,
  Or if, at times, its beams
Come on the memory, they pass o'er
  Like shadows in our dreams.

IV.

But when that flame has blazed into
  A being and a power,
And smiled in scorn upon the dew
  That fell in its first warm hour,
'Tis the flame that curls round the martyr's head,
  Whose task is to destroy;
'Tis the lamp on the altars of the dead,
  Whose light but darkens joy.

V.

Then crush, even in their hour of birth,
  The infant buds of Love,
And tread his glowing fire to earth,
  Ere 'tis dark in clouds above;
Cherish no more a cypress-tree
  To shade thy future years,
Nor nurse a heart-flame that may be
  Quenched only with thy tears.

A SKETCH.

Her Leghorn hat was of the bright gold tint
The setting sunbeams give to autumn clouds;
The riband that encircled it as blue
As spots of sky upon a moonless night,
When stars are keeping revelry in heaven;
A single ringlet of her clustering hair
Fell gracefully beneath her hat, in curls
As dark as down upon the raven's wing;
The kerchief, partly o'er her shoulders flung,
And partly waving in the wind, was woven

Of every color the first rainbow wore,
When it came smiling in its hues of beauty,
A promise from on high to a lost world.
Her robe seemed of the snow just fallen to earth,
Pure from its home in the far winter clouds,
As white, as stainless; and around her waist
(You might have spanned it with your thumb and
finger),
A girdle of the hue of Indian pearls
Was twined, resembling the faint line of water
That follows the swift bark o'er quiet seas.
Her face I saw not: but her shape, her form,
Was one of those with which creating bards
People a world of their own fashioning,
Forms for the heart to love and cherish ever,
The visiting angels of our twilight dreams.
Her foot was loveliest of remembered things,
Small as a fairy's on a moonlit leaf
Listening the wind-harp's song, and watching by
The wild-thyme pillow of her sleeping queen,

When proud Titania shuns her Oberon.
But 'twas that foot which broke the spell—alas!
Its stocking had a deep, deep tinge of blue—
I turned away in sadness, and passed on.

DOMESTIC HAPPINESS.

. . . . The only bliss
Of Paradise that has survived the fall.

COWPER.

I.

"BESIDE the nuptial curtain bright,"
The Bard of Eden sings,
"Young Love his constant lamp will light,
And wave his purple wings."
But rain-drops from the clouds of care
May bid that lamp be dim,
And the boy Love will pout and swear
'Tis then no place for him.

II.

So mused the lovely Mrs. Dash;
  'Tis wrong to mention names;
When for her surly husband's cash
  She urged in vain her claims.
"I want a little money, dear,
  For Vandervoort and Flandin,
Their bill, which now has run a year,
  To-morrow mean to hand in."

III.

"More?" cried the husband, half asleep,
  "You'll drive me to despair;"
The lady was too proud to weep,
  And too polite to swear.
She bit her lip for very spite,
  He felt a storm was brewing,
And dreamed of nothing else all night,
  But brokers, banks, and ruin.

IV.

He thought her pretty once, but dreams
  Have sure a wondrous power,
For to his eye the lady seems
  Quite altered since that hour;
And Love, who, on their bridal eve,
  Had promised long to stay,
Forgot his promise, took French leave,
  And bore his lamp away.

MAGDALEN.[7]

I.

A sword, whose blade has ne'er been wet
  With blood, except of freedom's foes;
That hope which, though its sun be set,
  Still with a starlight beauty glows;
A heart that worshipp'd in Romance
  The Spirit of the buried Time,
And dreams of knight, and steed, and lance,
  And ladye-love, and minstrel-rhyme;
These had been, and I deemed would be
My joy, whate'er my destiny.

II.

Born in a camp, its watch-fires bright
  Alone illumed my cradle-bed;
And I had borne with wild delight
  My banner where Bolivar led,
Ere manhood's hue was on my cheek,
  Or manhood's pride was on my brow.
Its folds are furled—the war-bird's beak
  Is thirsty on the Andes now;
I longed, like her, for other skies
Clouded by Glory's sacrifice.

III.

In Greece, the brave heart's Holy Land,
  Its soldier-song the bugle sings;
And I had buckled on my brand,
  And waited but the sea-wind's wings,
To bear me where, or lost or won
  Her battle, in its frown or smile,

Men live with those of Marathon,
  Or die with those of Scio's isle;
And find in Valor's tent or tomb,
In life or death, a glorious home.

IV.

I could have left but yesterday
  The scene of my boy-years behind,
And floated on my careless way
  Wherever willed the breathing wind.
I could have bade adieu to aught
  I've sought, or met, or welcomed here,
Without an hour of shaded thought,
  A sigh, a murmur, or a tear.
Such was I yesterday—but then
I had not known thee, Magdalen.

V.

To-day there is a change within me,
There is a weight upon my brow,
And Fame, whose whispers once could win me
From all I loved, is powerless now.
There ever is a form, a face
Of maiden beauty in my dreams,
Speeding before me, like the race
To ocean of the mountain streams—
With dancing hair, and laughing eyes,
That seem to mock me as it flies.

VI.

My sword—it slumbers in its sheath;
My hopes—their starry light is gone;
My heart—the fabled clock of death
Beats with the same low, lingering tone:
And this, the land of Magdalen,
Seems now the only spot on earth

Where skies are blue and flowers are green;
And here I'd build my household hearth,
And breathe my song of joy, and twine
A lovely being's name with mine.

VII.

In vain! in vain! the sail is spread;
To sea! to sea! my task is there;
But when among the unmourned dead
They lay me, and the ocean air
Brings tidings of my day of doom,
Mayst thou be then, as now thou art,
The load-star of a happy home;
In smile and voice, in eye and heart
The same as thou hast ever been,
The loved, the lovely Magdalen

FROM THE ITALIAN.

Eyes with the same blue witchery as those
Of Psyche, which caught Love in his own wiles;
Lips of the breath and hue of the red rose,
That move but with kind words and sweetest smiles;
A power of motion and of look, whose art
Throws, silently, around the wildest heart
The net it would not break; a form which vies
With that the Grecian imaged in his mind,
And gazed upon in dreams, and sighed to find
His breathing marble could not realize.

Know ye this picture? There is one alone
Can call its pencilled lineaments her own.
She whom, at morning, when the summer air
Wanders, delighted, o'er her face of flowers,
And lingers in the ringlets of her hair,
We deem the Hebe of Jove's banquet hours;
She who, at evening, when her fingers press
The harp, and wake its harmonies divine,
Seems sweetest-voiced and loveliest of the Nine,
The minstrel of the bowers of happiness,
She whom the Graces nurtured—at her birth,
The sea-born Goddess and the Huntress maid,
Beings whose beauty is not of the earth,
Came from their myrtle home and forest shade,
Blending immortal joy with mortal mirth:
And Dian said, "Fair sister, be she mine
In her heart's purity, in beauty thine."
The smiling infant listened and obeyed.

TRANSLATION

FROM THE GERMAN OF GOETHE.

AGAIN ye come, again ye throng around me,
  Dim, shadowy beings of my boyhood's dream!
Still shall I bless, as then, your spell that bound me?
  Still bend to mists and vapors as ye seem?
Nearer ye come: I yield me as ye found me
  In youth, your worshipper; and as the stream
Of air that folds you in its magic wreaths,
Flows by my lips, youth's joy my bosom breathes.

Lost forms and loved ones ye are with you bringing,
  And dearest images of happier days,
First-love and friendship in your path upspringing,
  Like old tradition's half-remembered lays,
And long-slept sorrows waked, whose dirge-like singing
  Recalls my life's strange labyrinthine maze,
And names the heart-mourned many a stern doom,
Ere their year's summer, summoned to the tomb.

They hear not these my last songs, they whose greeting
  Gladdened my first; my spring-time friends have gone,
And gone, fast journeying from that place of meeting,
  The echoes of their welcome, one by one.
Though stranger crowds, my listeners since, are beating
  Time to my music, their applauding tone
More grieves than glads me, while the tried and true,
If yet on earth, are wandering far and few.

A longing long unfelt, a deep-drawn sighing
  For the far Spirit-World o'erpowers me now;
My song's faint voice sinks fainter, like the dying
  Tones of the wind-harp swinging from the bough,
And my changed heart throbs warm, no more denying
  Tears to my eyes, or sadness to my brow:
The near afar off seems, the distant nigh,
The now a dream, the past reality.

WOMAN.

WRITTEN IN THE ALBUM OF AN UNKNOWN LADY.

Lady, although we have not met,
  And may not meet, beneath the sky;
And whether thine are eyes of jet,
Gray, or dark blue, or violet,
  Or hazel—heaven knows, not I;

Whether around thy cheek of rose
  A maiden's glowing locks are curled,
And to some thousand kneeling beaux,
Thy frown is cold as winter's snows,
  Thy smile is worth a world;

Or whether, past youth's joyous strife,
  The calm of thought is on thy brow,
And thou art in thy noon of life,
Loving and loved, a happy wife,
  And happier mother now,

I know not: but, whate'er thou art,
  Whoe'er thou art, were mine the spell,
To call Fate's joys or blunt his dart,
There should not be one hand or heart
  But served or wished thee well.

For thou art Woman—with that word
  Life's dearest hopes and memories come,
Truth, Beauty, Love—in her adored,
And earth's lost Paradise restored
  In the green bower of home.

What is man's love? His vows are broke,
  Even while his parting kiss is warm;
But woman's love all change will mock,
And, like the ivy round the oak,
  Cling closest in the storm.

And well the Poet at her shrine
  May bend, and worship while he woos;
To him she is a thing divine,
The inspiration of his line,
  His loved one and his Muse.

If to his song the echo rings
  Of Fame—'tis woman's voice he hears;
If ever from his lyre's proud strings
Flow sounds like rush of angel wings,
'Tis that she listens while he sings,
  With blended smiles and tears:

Smiles—tears—whose blessed and blessing power,
  Like sun and dew o'er summer's tree,
Alone keeps green through Time's long hour,
That frailer thing than leaf or flower,
  A Poet's immortality.

1824.

A POET'S DAUGHTER.

FOR THE ALBUM OF MISS * * *, AT THE REQUEST OF HER FATHER.

"A Lady asks the Minstrel's rhyme."
A Lady asks? There was a time
When, musical as play-bell's chime
To wearied boy,
That sound would summon dreams sublime
Of pride and joy.

But now the spell hath lost its sway,
Life's first-born fancies first decay,
Gone are the plumes and pennons gay
  Of young Romance;
There linger but her ruins gray,
  And broken lance.

'Tis a new world—no more to maid,
Warrior, or bard, is homage paid;
The bay-tree's, laurel's, myrtle's shade,
  Men's thoughts resign;
Heaven placed us here to vote and trade,
  Twin tasks divine!

"'Tis youth, 'tis beauty asks; the green
And growing leaves of seventeen
Are round her; and, half hid, half seen,
  A violet flower,
Nursed by the virtues she hath been
  From childhood's hour."

Blind passion's picture—yet for this
We woo the life-long bridal kiss,
And blend our every hope of bliss
  With hers we love;
Unmindful of the serpent's hiss
  In Eden's grove.

Beauty—the fading rainbow's pride,
Youth—'twas the charm of her who died
At dawn, and by her coffin's side
  A grandsire stands,
Age-strengthened, like the oak storm-tried
  Of mountain lands.

Youth's coffin—hush the tale it tells,
Be silent, memory's funeral bells!
Lone in one heart, her home, it dwells
  Untold till death,
And where the grave-mound greenly swells
  O'er buried faith.

"But what if hers are rank and power,
Armies her train, a throne her bower,
A kingdom's gold her marriage dower,
Broad seas and lands?
What if from bannered hall and tower
A queen commands?"

A queen? Earth's regal moons have set.
Where perished Marie Antoinette?
Where's Bordeaux's mother? Where the jet-
Black Haytian dame?
And Lusitania's coronet?
And Angoulême?

Empires to-day are upside down,
The castle kneels before the town,
The monarch fears a printer's frown,
A brickbat's range;
Give me, in preference to a crown,
Five shillings change.

"But her who asks, though first among
The good, the beautiful, the young,
The birthright of a spell more strong
Than these hath brought her;
She is your kinswoman in song,
A Poet's daughter."

A Poet's daughter? Could I claim
The consanguinity of fame,
Veins of my intellectual frame!
Your blood would glow
Proudly to sing that gentlest name
Of aught below.

A Poet's daughter—dearer word
Lip hath not spoke nor listener heard,
Fit theme for song of bee and bird
From morn till even,
And wind-harp by the breathing stirred
Of star-lit heaven.

My spirit's wings are weak, the fire
Poetic comes but to expire,
Her name needs not my humble lyre
  To bid it live;
She hath already from her sire
  All bard can give.

1831.

CONNECTICUT.

FROM AN UNPUBLISHED POEM.

"The woods in which we had dwelt pleasantly rustled their green leaves in the song, and our streams were there with the sound of all their waters."

MONTROSE.

I.

—— still her gray rocks tower above the sea
  That crouches at their feet, a conquered wave;
'Tis a rough land of earth, and stone, and tree,
  Where breathes no castled lord or cabined slave;
Where thoughts, and tongues, and hands are bold and free,
  And friends will find a welcome, foes a grave;
And where none kneel, save when to heaven they pray,
Nor even then, unless in their own way.

II.

Theirs is a pure republic, wild, yet strong,
  A "fierce democracie," where all are true
To what themselves have voted—right or wrong—
  And to their laws denominated blue;
(If red, they might to Draco's code belong;)
  A vestal state, which power could not subdue,
Nor promise win—like her own eagle's nest,
Sacred—the San Marino of the West.

III.

A justice of the peace, for the time being,
  They bow to, but may turn him out next year;
They reverence their priest, but disagreeing
  In price or creed, dismiss him without fear;
They have a natural talent for foreseeing
  And knowing all things; and should Park appear
From his long tour in Africa, to show
The Niger's source, they'd meet him with—we know.

IV.

They love their land, because it is their own,
And scorn to give aught other reason why;
Would shake hands with a king upon his throne,
And think it kindness to his majesty;
A stubborn race, fearing and flattering none.
Such are they nurtured, such they live and die:
All—but a few apostates, who are meddling
With merchandise, pounds, shillings, pence, and peddling;

V.

Or wandering through the southern countries, teaching
The A B C from Webster's spelling-book;
Gallant and godly, making love and preaching,
And gaining, by what they call "hook and crook,"
And what the moralists call over-reaching,
A decent living. The Virginians look
Upon them with as favorable eyes
As Gabriel on the devil in paradise.

VI.

But these are but their outcasts. View them near
  At home, where all their worth and pride is placed;
And there their hospitable fires burn clear,
  And there the lowliest farmhouse hearth is graced
With manly hearts, in piety sincere,
  Faithful in love, in honor stern and chaste,
In friendship warm and true, in danger brave,
Beloved in life, and sainted in the grave.

VII.

And minds have there been nurtured, whose control
  Is felt even in their nation's destiny;
Men who swayed senates with a statesman's soul,
  And looked on armies with a leader's eye;
Names that adorn and dignify the scroll,
  Whose leaves contain their country's history,
And tales of love and war—listen to one
Of the Green-Mountaineer—the Stark of Bennington.

VIII.

When on that field his band the Hessians fought,
Briefly he spoke before the fight began:
"Soldiers! those German gentlemen are bought
For four pounds eight and sevenpence per man,
By England's king; a bargain, as is thought.
Are we worth more? Let's prove it now we can;
For we must beat them, boys, ere set of sun,
Or Mary Stark's a widow." It was done.

IX.

Hers are not Tempe's nor Arcadia's spring,
Nor the long summer of Cathayan vales,
The vines, the flowers, the air, the skies, that fling
Such wild enchantment o'er Boccaccio's tales
Of Florence and the Arno; yet the wing
Of life's best angel, Health, is on her gales
Through sun and snow; and in the autumn time
Earth has no purer and no lovelier clime.

X.

Her clear, warm heaven at noon—the mist that shrouds
Her twilight hills—her cool and starry eves,
The glorious splendor of her sunset clouds,
The rainbow beauty of her forest leaves,
Come o'er the eye, in solitude and crowds,
Where'er his web of song her poet weaves;
And his mind's brightest vision but displays
The autumn scenery of his boyhood's days.

XI.

And when you dream of woman, and her love;
Her truth, her tenderness, her gentle power;
The maiden, listening in the moonlight grove,
The mother smiling in her infant's bower;
Forms, features, worshipped while we breathe or move,
Be by some spirit of your dreaming hour
Borne, like Loretto's chapel, through the air
To the green land I sing, then wake, you'll find them there.

MUSIC.

TO A BOY OF FOUR YEARS OLD, ON HEARING HIM PLAY ON THE HARP.

Sweet boy! before thy lips can learn
  In speech thy wishes to make known,
Are "thoughts that breathe and words that burn"
  Heard in thy music's tone.

Were Genius tasked to prove the might,
  The magic of her hidden spell,
She well might name thee with delight
  As her own miracle.

Who that hath heard, from summer trees,
The sweet wild song of summer birds,
When morning to the far-off breeze
Whispers her bidding words;

Or listened to the bird of night,
The minstrel of the starlight hours,
Companion of the firefly's flight,
Cool dews, and closed flowers;

But deemed that spirits of the air
Had left their native homes in heaven,
And that the music warbled there
To earth a while was given?

For with that music came the thought
That life's young purity was theirs,
And love, all artless and untaught,
Breathed in their woodland airs.

And when, sweet boy! thy baby fingers
  Wake sounds of heaven's own harmony,
How welcome is the thought that lingers
  Upon thy lyre and thee!

It calls up visions of past days,
  When life was infancy and song
To us, and old remembered lays,
  Unheard, unheeded long;

Revive in joy or grief within us,
  Like lost friends wakened from their sleep,
With all their early power to win us
  Alike to smile or weep.

And when we gaze upon that face,
  Blooming in innocence and truth,
And mark its dimpled artlessness,
  Its beauty and its youth;

We think of better worlds than this,
  Of other beings pure as thou,
Who breathe, on winds of Paradise,
  Music as thine is now.

And know the only emblem meet
  Of that pure Faith the heart adores,
To be a child like thee, whose feet
  Are strangers on Life's shores.

ON THE DEATH OF

LIEUT. WILLIAM HOWARD ALLEN,[9]

OF THE AMERICAN NAVY.

He hath been mourned as brave men mourn the brave,
And wept as nations weep their cherished dead,
With bitter, but proud tears, and o'er his head
The eternal flowers whose root is in the grave,
The flowers of Fame, are beautiful and green;
And by his grave's side pilgrim feet have been,
And blessings, pure as men to martyrs give,
Have there been breathed by those he died to save.
—Pride of his country's banded chivalry,
His fame their hope, his name their battle cry;
He lived as mothers wish their sons to live,
He died as fathers wish their sons to die.

If on the grief-worn cheek the hues of bliss,
Which fade when all we love is in the tomb,
Could ever know on earth a second bloom,
The memory of a gallant death like his
Would call them into being; but the few,
Who as their friend, their brother, or their son,
His kind warm heart and gentle spirit knew,
Had long lived, hoped, and feared for him alone;
His voice their morning music, and his eye
The only starlight of their evening sky,
Till even the sun of happiness seemed dim,
And life's best joys were sorrows but with him;
And when, the burning bullet in his breast,
He dropped, like summer fruit from off the bough,
There was one heart that knew and loved him best—
It was a mother's—and is broken now.

FANNY.

"A fairy vision
Of some gay creatures of the element,
That in the colors of the rainbow live,
And play in the plighted clouds."

MILTON.

FANNY.

I.

FANNY was younger once than she is now,
  And prettier of course: I do not mean
To say that there are wrinkles on her brow;
  Yet, to be candid, she is past eighteen—
Perhaps past twenty—but the girl is shy
About her age, and Heaven forbid that I

II.

Should get myself in trouble by revealing
A secret of this sort; I have too long
Loved pretty women with a poet's feeling,
And when a boy, in day dream and in song,
Have knelt me down and worshipped them: alas!
They never thanked me for 't—but let that pass.

III.

I've felt full many a heart-ache in my day,
At the mere rustling of a muslin gown,
And caught some dreadful colds, I blush to say,
While shivering in the shade of beauty's frown.
They say her smiles are sunbeams—it may be—
But never a sunbeam would she throw on me.

IV.

But Fanny's is an eye that you may gaze on
  For half an hour, without the slightest harm;
E'en when she wore her smiling summer face on
  There was but little danger, and the charm
That youth and wealth once gave, has bade farewell.
Hers is a sad, sad tale—'tis mine its woes to tell.

V.

Her father kept, some fifteen years ago,
  A retail dry-good shop in Chatham-street,
And nursed his little earnings, sure though slow,
  Till, having mustered wherewithal to meet
The gaze of the great world, he breathed the air
Of Pearl-street—and "set up" in Hanover-square.

VI.

Money is power, 'tis said—I never tried;
I'm but a poet—and bank-notes to me
Are curiosities, as closely eyed,
Whene'er I get them, as a stone would be,
Tossed from the moon on Doctor Mitchill's table,
Or classic brickbat from the tower of Babel.

VII.

But he I sing of well has known and felt
That money hath a power and a dominion;
For when in Chatham-street the good man dwelt,
No one would give a *sous* for his opinion.
And though his neighbors were extremely civil,
Yet, on the whole, they thought him—a poor devil,

VIII.

A decent kind of person; one whose head
  Was not of brains particularly full;
It was not known that he had ever said
  Any thing worth repeating—'twas a dull,
Good, honest man—what Paulding's muse would call
A "cabbage head"—but he excelled them all

IX.

In that most noble of the sciences,
  The art of making money; and he found
The zeal for quizzing him grew less and less,
  As he grew richer; till upon the ground
Of Pearl-street, treading proudly in the might
And majesty of wealth, a sudden light

X.

Flashed like the midnight lightning on the eyes
  Of all who knew him; brilliant traits of mind,
And genius, clear and countless as the dies
  Upon the peacock's plumage; taste refined,
Wisdom and wit, were his—perhaps much more.
'Twas strange they had not found it out before.

XI.

In this quick transformation, it is true
  That cash had no small share; but there were still
Some other causes, which then gave a new
  Impulse to head and heart, and joined to fill
His brain with knowledge; for there first he met
The editor of the New-York Gazette,

XII.

The sapient Mr. L**G. The world of him
Knows much, yet not one half so much as he
Knows of the world. Up to its very brim
The goblet of his mind is sparkling free
With lore and learning. Had proud Sheba's queen,
In all her bloom and beauty, but have seen

XIII.

This modern Solomon, the Israelite,
Earth's monarch as he was, had never won her.
He would have hanged himself for very spite,
And she, blessed woman, might have had the honor
Of some neat "paragraphs"—worth all the lays
That Judah's minstrel warbled in her praise.

XIV.

Her star arose too soon; but that which swayed
  Th' ascendant at our merchant's natal hour
Was bright with better destiny—its aid
  Led him to pluck within the classic bower
Of bulletins, the blossoms of true knowledge;
And L**G supplied the loss of school and college.

XV.

For there he learned the news some minutes sooner
  Than others could; and to distinguish well
The different signals, whether ship or schooner,
  Hoisted at Staten Island; and to tell
The change of wind, and of his neighbor's fortunes,
And, best of all—he there learned self-importance.

XVI.

Nor were these all the advantages derived
  From change of scene; for near his domicil
He of the pair of polished lamps then lived,
  And in my hero's promenades, at will,
Could he behold them burning—and their flame
Kindled within his breast the love of fame,

XVII.

And politics, and country; the pure glow
  Of patriot ardor, and the consciousness
That talents such as his might well bestow
  A lustre on the city; she would bless
His name; and that some service should be done her,
He pledged "life, fortune, and his sacred honor."

XVIII.

And when the sounds of music and of mirth,
Bursting from Fashion's groups assembled there,
Were heard, as round their lone plebeian hearth
Fanny and he were seated—he would dare
To whisper fondly, that the time might come
When he and his could give as brilliant routs at home.

XIX.

And oft would Fanny near that mansion linger,
When the cold winter moon was high in heaven,
And trace out, by the aid of Fancy's finger,
Cards for some future party, to be given
When she, in turn, should be a *belle*, and they
Had lived their little hour, and passed away.

XX.

There are some happy moments in this lone
  And desolate world of ours, that well repay
The toil of struggling through it, and atone
  For many a long, sad night and weary day.
They come upon the mind like some wild air
Of distant music, when we know not where,

XXI.

Or whence, the sounds are brought from, and their power,
  Though brief, is boundless. That far, future home,
Oft dreamed of, beckons near—its rose-wreathed bower,
  And cloudless skies before us: we become
Changed on the instant—all gold leaf and gilding:
This is, in vulgar phrase, called "castle building."

XXII.

But these, like sunset clouds, fade soon; 'tis vain
  To bid them linger longer, or to ask
On what day they intend to call again;
  And, surely, 'twere a philosophic task,
Worthy a Mitchill, in his hours of leisure,
To find some means to summon them at pleasure.

XXIII.

There certainly are powers of doing this,
  In some degree at least—for instance, drinking.
Champagne will bathe the heart a while in bliss,
  And keep the head a little time from thinking
Of cares or creditors—the best wine in town
You'll get from Lynch—the cash must be paid down.

XXIV.

But if you are a bachelor, like me,
  And spurn all chains, even though made of roses,
I'd recommend segars—there is a free
  And happy spirit, that, unseen, reposes
On the dim shadowy clouds that hover o'er you,
When smoking quietly with a warm fire before you.

XXV.

Dear to the exile is his native land,
  In memory's twilight beauty seen afar:
Dear to the broker is a note of hand,
  Collaterally secured—the polar star
Is dear at midnight to the sailor's eyes,
And dear are Bristed's volumes at "half price;"

XXVI.

But dearer far to me each fairy minute
  Spent in that fond forgetfulness of grief;
There is an airy web of magic in it,
  As in Othello's pocket-handkerchief,
Veiling the wrinkles on the brow of sorrow,
The gathering gloom to-day, the thunder-cloud to-morrow.

XXVII.

And these are innocent thoughts—a man may sit
  Upon a bright throne of his own creation;
Untortured by the ghastly sprites that flit
  Around the many, whose exalted station
Has been attained by means 'twere pain to hint on,
Just for the rhyme's sake—instance Mr. Cl*n*on.

XXVIII.

He struggled hard, but not in vain, and breathes
  The mountain air at last; but there are others
Who strove, like him, to win the glittering wreaths
  Of power, his early partisans and brothers,
That linger yet in dust from whence they sprung,
Unhonored and unpaid, though, luckily, unhung.

XXIX.

'Twas theirs to fill with gas the huge balloon
  Of party; and they hoped, when it arose,
To soar like eagles in the blaze of noon,
  Above the gaping crowd of friends and foes.
Alas! like Guillé's car, it soared without them,
And left them with a mob to jeer and flout them.

XXX.

Though Fanny's moonlight dreams were sweet as those
  I've dwelt so long upon—they were more stable;
Hers were not "castles in the air" that rose
  Based upon nothing; for her sire was able,
As well she knew, to "buy out" the one half
Of Fashion's glittering train, that nightly quaff

XXXI.

Wine, wit, and wisdom, at a midnight rout,
  From dandy coachmen, whose "exquisite" grin
And "ruffian" lounge flash brilliantly without,
  Down to their brother dandies ranged within,
Gay as the Brussels carpeting they tread on,
And sapient as the oysters they are fed on.

XXXII.

And Rumor (she's a famous liar, yet
'Tis wonderful how easy we believe her)
Had whispered he was rich, and all he met
In Wall-street, nodded, smiled, and "tipped the beaver;"
All,—from Mr. Gelston, the collector,
Down to the broker, and the bank director.

XXXIII.

A few brief years passed over, and his rank
Among the worthies of that street was fixed;
He had become director of a bank,
And six insurance offices, and mixed
Familiarly, as one among his peers,
With grocers, dry-good merchants, auctioneers,

XXXIV.

Brokers of all grades—stock and pawn—and Jews
  Of all religions, who at noonday form,
On 'Change, that brotherhood the moral muse
  Delights in, where the heart is pure and warm,
And each exerts his intellectual force
To cheat his neighbor—legally, of course.

XXXV.

And there he shone a planetary star,
  Circled around by lesser orbs, whose beams
From his were borrowed. The simile is not far
  From truth—for many bosom friends, it seems,
Did borrow of him, and sometimes forget
To pay—indeed, they have not paid him yet.

XXXVI.

But these he deemed as trifles, when each mouth
Was open in his praise, and plaudits rose
Upon his willing ear, "like the sweet south
Upon a bank of violets," from those
Who knew his talents, virtues, and so forth;
That is—knew how much money he was worth.

XXXVII.

Alas! poor human nature; had he been
But satisfied with this, his golden days
Their setting hour of darkness had not seen,
And he might still (in the mercantile phrase)
Be living "in good order and condition;"
But he was ruined by that jade Ambition,

XXXVIII.

"That last infirmity of noble minds,"
Whose spell, like whiskey, your true patriot liquor,
To politics the lofty hearts inclines
Of all, from Clinton down to the bill-sticker
Of a ward-meeting. She came slyly creeping
To his bedside, where he lay snug and sleeping.

XXXIX.

Her brow was turbaned with a bucktail wreath,
A broach of terrapin her bosom wore,
Tompkins's letter was just seen beneath
Her arm, and in her hand on high she bore
A National Advocate—Pell's polite Review
Lay at her feet—'twas pommelled black and blue.

XL.

She was in fashion's elegant undress,
Muffled from throat to ankle; and her hair
Was all "*en papillotes*," each auburn tress
Prettily pinned apart. You well might swear
She was no beauty; yet, when "made up," ready
For visiters, 'twas quite another lady.

XLI.

Since that wise pedant, Johnson, was in fashion,
Manners have changed as well as moons; and he
Would fret himself once more into a passion,
Should he return (which heaven forbid!), and see,
How strangely from his standard dictionary,
The meaning of some words is made to vary.

XLII.

For instance, an *undress* at present means
  The wearing a pelisse, a shawl, or so;
Or any thing you please, in short, that screens
  The face, and hides the form from top to toe;
Of power to brave a quizzing-glass, or storm—
'Tis worn in summer, when the weather's warm.

XLIII.

But a full dress is for a winter's night.
  The most genteel is made of "woven air;"
That kind of classic cobweb, soft and light,
  Which Lady Morgan's Ida used to wear.
And ladies, this aërial manner dressed in,
Look Eve-like, angel-like, and interesting.

XLIV.

But Miss Ambition was, as I was saying,
"*Dèshabillée*"—his bedside tripping near,
And, gently on his nose her fingers laying,
She roared out Tammany! in his frighted ear.
The potent word awoke him from his nap,
And then she vanished, whispering *verbum sap.*

XLV.

The last words were beyond his comprehension,
For he had left off schooling, ere the Greek
Or Latin classics claimed his mind's attention:
Besides, he often had been heard to speak
Contemptuously of all that sort of knowledge,
Taught so profoundly in Columbia College.

XLVI.

We owe the ancients something. You have read
  Their works, no doubt—at least in a translation;
Yet there was argument in what he said,
  I scorn equivocation or evasion,
And own it must, in candor, be confessed,
They were an ignorant set of men at best.

XLVII.

'Twas their misfortune to be born too soon
  By centuries, and in the wrong place too;
They never saw a steamboat, or balloon,
  Velocipede, or Quarterly Review;
Or wore a pair of Baehr's black satin breeches,
Or read an Almanac, or Clinton's Speeches.

XLVIII.

In short, in every thing we far outshine them,—
Art, science, taste, and talent; and a stroll
Through this enlightened city would refine them
More than ten years hard study of the whole
Their genius has produced of rich and rare—
God bless the Corporation and the Mayor!

XLIX.

In sculpture, we've a grace the Grecian master,
Blushing, had owned his purest model lacks;
We've Mr. Bogart in the best of plaster,
The Witch of Endor in the best of wax,
Besides the head of Franklin on the roof
Of Mr. Lang, both jest and weather proof.

L.

And on our City Hall a Justice stands;
  A neater form was never made of board,
Holding majestically in her hands
  A pair of steelyards and a wooden sword;
And looking down with complaisant civility—
Emblem of dignity and durability.

LI.

In painting, we have Trumbull's proud *chef d'œuvre*,
  Blending in one the funny and the fine:
His "Independence" will endure forever,
  And so will Mr. Allen's lottery sign;
And all that grace the Academy of Arts,
From Dr. Hosack's face to Bonaparte's.

LII.

In architecture, our unrivalled skill
  Cullen's magnesian shop has loudly spoken
To an admiring world; and better still
  Is Gautier's fairy palace at Hoboken.
In music, we've the Euterpian Society,
And amateurs, a wonderful variety.

LIII.

In physic, we have Francis and M'Neven,
  Famed for long heads, short lectures, and long bills;
And Quackenboss and others, who from heaven
  Were rained upon us in a shower of pills;
They'd beat the deathless Esculapius hollow,
And make a starveling druggist of Apollo.

LIV.

And who, that ever slumbered at the Forum,
　But owns the first of orators we claim;
Cicero would have bowed the knee before 'em—
　And for law eloquence, we've Doctor Graham.
Compared with him, their Justins and Quintillians
Had dwindled into second-rate civilians.

LV.

For purity and chastity of style,
　There's Pell's preface, and puffs by Horne and Waite.
For penetration deep, and learned toil,
　And all that stamps an author truly great,
Have we not Bristed's ponderous tomes? a treasure
For any man of patience and of leisure.

LVI.

Oxonian Bristed! many a foolscap page
  He, in his time, hath written, and moreover
(What few will do in this degenerate age)
  Hath read his own works, as you may discover
By counting his quotations from himself—
You'll find the books on any auction shelf.

LVII.

I beg Great Britain's pardon; 'tis not meant
  To claim this Oxford scholar as our own:
That he was shipped off here to represent
  Her literature among us, is well known;
And none could better fill the lofty station
Of Learning's envoy from the British nation.

LVIII.

We fondly hope that he will be respected
  At home, and soon obtain a place or pension.
We should regret to see him live neglected,
  Like Fearon, Ashe, and others we could mention;
Who paid us friendly visits to abuse
Our country, and find food for the reviews.

LIX.

But to return.—The Heliconian waters
  Are sparkling in their native fount no more,
And after years of wandering, the nine daughters
  Of poetry have found upon our shore
A happier home, and on their sacred shrines
Glow in immortal ink, the polished lines

LX.

Of Woodworth, Doctor Farmer, Moses Scott—
  Names hallowed by their reader's sweetest smile;
And who that reads at all has read them not?
  "That blind old man of Scio's rocky isle,"
Homer, was well enough; but would he ever
Have written, think ye, the Backwoodsman? never.

LXI.

Alas! for Paulding—I regret to see
  In such a stanza one whose giant powers,
Seen in their native element, will be
  Known to a future age, the pride of ours.
There is none breathing who can better wield
The battle-axe of satire. On its field

LXII.

The wreath he fought for he has bravely won,
  Long be its laurel green around his brow!
It is too true, I'm somewhat fond of fun
  And jesting; but for once I'm serious now.
Why is he sipping weak Castalian dews?
The muse has damned him—let him damn the muse.

LXIII.

But to return once more: the ancients fought
  Some tolerable battles. Marathon
Is still a theme for high and holy thought,
  And many a poet's lay. We linger on
The page that tells us of the brave and free,
And reverence thy name, unmatched Thermopylæ.

LXIV.

And there were spirited troops in other days—
  The Roman legion and the Spartan band,
And Swartwout's gallant corps, the Iron Grays—
  Soldiers who met their foemen hand to hand,
Or swore, at least, to meet them undismayed;
Yet what were these to General Laight's brigade

LXV.

Of veterans? nursed in that Free School of glory,
  The New-York State Militia. From Bellevue,
E'en to the Battery flagstaff, the proud story
  Of their manœuvres at the last review
Has rang; and Clinton's "order" told afar
He never led a better corps to war.

LXVI.

What, Egypt, was thy magic, to the tricks
  Of Mr. Charles, Judge Spencer, or Van Buren?
The first with cards, the last in politics,
  A conjuror's fame for years have been securing.
And who would now the Athenian dramas read
When he can get "Wall-street," by Mr. Mead.

LXVII.

I might say much about our lettered men,
  Those "grave and reverend seigniors," who compose
Our learned societies—but here my pen
  Stops short; for they themselves, the rumor goes,
The exclusive privilege by patent claim,
Of trumpeting (as the phrase is) their own fame.

LXVIII.

And, therefore, I am silent. It remains
  To bless the hour the Corporation took it
Into their heads to give the rich in brains,
  The worn-out mansion of the poor in pocket,
Once "the old almshouse," now a school of wisdom,
Sacred to Scudder's shells and Dr. Griscom.

LXIX.

But whither am I wandering? The esteem
  I bear "this fair city of the heart,"
To me a dear enthusiastic theme,
  Has forced me, all unconsciously, to part
Too long from him, the hero of my story.
Where was he?—waking from his dream of glory.

LXX.

And she, the lady of his dream, had fled,
And left him somewhat puzzled and confused.
He understood, however, half she said;
And that is quite as much as we are used
To comprehend, or fancy worth repeating,
In speeches heard at any public meeting.

LXXI.

And the next evening found him at the Hall;
There he was welcomed by the cordial hand,
And met the warm and friendly grasp of all
Who take, like watchmen, there, their nightly stand,
A ring, as in a boxing match, procuring,
To bet on Clinton, Tompkins, or Van Buren.

LXXII.

'Twas a propitious moment; for a while
  The waves of party were at rest. Upon
Each complacent brow was gay good humor's smile;
  And there was much of wit, and jest, and pun,
And high amid the circle, in great glee,
Sat Croaker's old acquaintance, John Targee.

LXXIII.

His jokes excelled the rest, and oft he sang
  Songs, patriotic, as in duty bound.
He had a little of the "nasal twang
  Heard at conventicle;" but yet you found
In him a dash of purity and brightness,
That spoke the man of taste and of politeness.

LXXIV.

For he had been, it seems, the bosom friend
  Of England's prettiest bard, Anacreon Moore.
They met when he, the bard, came here to lend
  His mirth and music to this favorite shore;
For, as the proverb saith, "birds of a feather
Instinctively will flock and fly together."

LXXV.

The winds that wave thy cedar boughs are breathing,
  "Lake of the Dismal Swamp!" that poet's name;
And the spray-showers their noonday halos wreathing
  Around "Cohoes," are brightened by his fame.
And bright its sunbeam o'er St. Lawrence smiles,
Her million lilies, and her thousand isles.

LXXVI.

We hear his music in her oarsmen's lay,
And where her church-bells "toll the evening chime;"
Yet when to him the grateful heart would pay
Its homage, now, and in all coming time,
Up springs a doubtful question whether we
Owe it to Tara's minstrel or Targee.

LXXVII.

Together oft they wandered—many a spot
Now consecrated, as the minstrel's theme,
By words of beauty ne'er to be forgot,
Their mutual feet have trod; and when the stream
Of thought and feeling flowed in mutual speech,
'Twere vain to tell how much each taught to each.

LXXVIII.

But, from the following song, it would appear
  That he of Erin from the sachem took
The model of his "Bower of Bendemeer,"
  One of the sweetest airs in Lalla Rookh;
'Tis to be hoped that in his next edition,
This, the original, will find admission.

SONG.

There's a barrel of porter at Tammany Hall,
  And the bucktails are swigging it all the night long;
In the time of my boyhood 'twas pleasant to call
  For a seat and segar, mid the jovial throng.

SONG.

There's a bower of roses by Bendemeer's stream,
And the nightingale sings round it all the night long;
In the time of my childhood 'twas like a sweet dream
To sit in the roses and hear the bird's song.

That beer and those bucktails I never forget;
But oft, when alone, and unnoticed by all,
I think, is the porter cask foaming there yet?
Are the bucktails still swigging at Tammany Hall?

No! the porter was out long before it was stale,
But some blossoms on many a nose brightly shone;
And the speeches inspired by the fumes of the ale,
Had the fragrance of porter when porter was gone.

How much Cozzens will draw of such beer ere he dies,
Is a question of moment to me and to all;
For still dear to my soul, as 'twas then to my eyes,
Is that barrel of porter at Tammany Hall.

That bower and its music I never forget;
  But oft, when alone, in the bloom of the year,
I think, is the nightingale singing there yet?
  Are the roses still bright by the calm Bendemeer?

No! the roses soon withered that hung o'er the wave,
  But some blossoms were gathered while freshly they shone;
And a dew was distilled from their flowers, that gave
  All the fragrance of summer when summer was gone.

Thus memory draws from delight ere it dies,
  An essence that breathes of it many a year;
Thus bright to my soul, as 'twas then to my eyes,
  Is that bower on the banks of the calm Bendemeer.

LXXIX.

For many months my hero ne'er neglected
 To take his ramble there, and soon found out,
In much less time than one could have expected,
 What 'twas they all were quarrelling about.
He learned the party countersigns by rote,
And when to clap his hands, and how to vote.

LXXX.

He learned that Clinton became Governor
 Somehow by chance, when we were all asleep;
That he had neither sense, nor talent, nor
 Any good quality, and would not keep
His place an hour after the next election—
So powerful was the voice of disaffection.

LXXXI.

That he was a mere puppet made to play
 A thousand tricks, while Spencer touched the springs—
Spencer, the mighty Warwick of his day,
 "That setter up, and puller down of kings,"
Aided by Miller, Pell, and Doctor Graham,
And other men of equal worth and fame.

LXXXII.

And that he'd set the people at defiance,
 By placing knaves and fools in public stations;
And that his works in literature and science
 Were but a schoolboy's web of misquotations;
And that he'd quoted from the devil even—
"Better to reign in hell than serve in heaven."

LXXXIII.

To these authentic facts each bucktail swore;
But Clinton's friends averred, in contradiction,
They were but fables, told by Mr. Noah,
Who had a privilege to deal in fiction,
Because he'd written travels, and a melo-
Drama; and was, withal, a pleasant fellow.

LXXXIV.

And they declared that Tompkins was no better
Than he should be; that he had borrowed money,
And paid it—not in cash—but with a letter;
And though some trifling service he had done, he
Still wanted spirit, energy, and fire;
And was disliked by—Mr. M'Intyre.

LXXXV.

In short, each one with whom in conversation
He joined, contrived to give him different views
Of men and measures; and the information
Which he obtained, but aided to confuse
His brain. At best, 'twas never very clear;
And now 'twas turned with politics and beer.

LXXXVI.

And he was puffed, and flattered, and caressed
By all, till he sincerely thought that nature
Had formed him for an alderman at least—
Perhaps, a member of the legislature;
And that he had the talents, ten times over,
Of H*n*y M**gs, or P*t*r H. W*nd*ver.

LXXXVII.

The man was mad, 'tis plain, and merits pity,
Or he had never dared, in such a tone,
To speak of two great persons, whom the city,
With pride and pleasure, points to as her own.
Men, wise in council, brilliant in debate,
"The expectancy and rose of the fair state."

LXXXVIII.

The one—for a pure style and classic manner,
Is—Mr. Sachem Mooney far before.
The other, in his speech about the banner,
Spell-bound his audience until they swore
That such a speech was never heard till then,
And never would be—till he spoke again.

LXXXIX.

Though 'twas presumptuous in this friend of ours
To think of rivalling these, I must allow
That still the man had talents; and the powers
Of his capacious intellect were now
Improved by foreign travel, and by reading,
And at the Hall he'd learned, of course, good breeding.

XC.

He had read the newspapers with great attention,
Advertisements and all; and Riley's book
Of travels—valued for its rich invention;
And Day and Turner's Price Current; and took
The Edinburgh and Quarterly Reviews;
And also Colonel Pell's; and, to amuse

XCI.

His leisure hours with classic tale and story,
  Longworth's Directory, and Mead's Wall-street,
And Mr. Delaplaine's Repository;
  And Mitchill's scientific works complete,
With other standard books of modern days,
Lay on his table, covered with green baize.

XCII.

His travels had extended to Bath races;
  And Bloomingdale and Bergen he had seen,
And Harlæm Heights; and many other places,
  By sea and land, had visited; and been,
In a steamboat of the Vice-President's,
To Staten-Island once—for fifty cents.

XCIII.

And he had dined, by special invitation,
  On turtle, with "the party" at Hoboken;
And thanked them for his card in an oration,
  Declared to be the shortest ever spoken.
And he had strolled one day o'er Weehawk hill:
A day worth all the rest—he recollects it still.

XCIV.

Weehawken! In thy mountain scenery yet,
  All we adore of nature in her wild
And frolic hour of infancy, is met;
  And never has a summer's morning smiled
Upon a lovelier scene, than the full eye
Of the enthusiast revels on—when high

XCV.

Amid thy forest solitudes, he climbs
O'er crags, that proudly tower above the deep,
And knows that sense of danger which sublimes
The breathless moment—when his daring step
Is on the verge of the cliff, and he can hear
The low dash of the wave with startled ear,

XCVI.

Like the death-music of his coming doom,
And clings to the green turf with desperate force,
As the heart clings to life; and when resume
The currents in his veins their wonted course,
There lingers a deep feeling—like the moan
Of wearied ocean, when the storm is gone.

XCVII.

In such an hour he turns, and on his view,
  Ocean, and earth, and heaven, burst before him;
Clouds slumbering at his feet, and the clear blue
  Of summer's sky in beauty bending o'er him—
The city bright below; and far away,
Sparkling in golden light, his own romantic bay.

XCVIII.

Tall spire, and glittering roof, and battlement,
  And banners floating in the sunny air;
And white sails o'er the calm blue waters bent,
  Green isle, and circling shore, are blended there
In wild reality. When life is old,
And many a scene forgot, the heart will hold

XCIX.

Its memory of this; nor lives there one
Whose infant breath was drawn, or boyhood's days
Of happiness were passed beneath that sun,
That in his manhood's prime can calmly gaze
Upon that bay, or on that mountain stand,
Nor feel the prouder of his native land.

C.

"This may be poetry, for aught I know,"
Said an old, worthy friend of mine, while leaning
Over my shoulder as I wrote, "although
I can't exactly comprehend its meaning.
For my part, I have long been a petitioner
To Mr. John M'Comb, the street-commissioner,

CI.

"That he would think of Weehawk, and would lay it
Handsomely out in avenue and square;
Then tax the land, and make its owners pay it
(As is the usual plan pursued elsewhere);
Blow up the rocks, and sell the wood for fuel—
'Twould save us many a dollar, and a duel."

CII.

The devil take you and John M'Comb, said I;
Lang, in its praise, has penned one paragraph,
And promised me another. I defy,
With such assistance, yours and the world's laugh;
And half believe that Paulding, on this theme,
Might be a poet—strange as it may seem.

CIII.

For even our traveller felt, when home returning
  From that day's tour, as on the deck he stood,
The fire of poetry within him burning;
  "Albeit unused to the rhyming mood;"
And with a pencil on his knee he wrote
The following flaming lines

TO THE HORSEBOAT.

1

Away—o'er the wave to the home we are seeking,
  Bark of my hope! ere the evening be gone;
There's a wild, wild note in the curlew's shrieking;
  There's a whisper of death in the wind's low moan.

2

Though blue and bright are the heavens above me,
And the stars are asleep on the quiet sea;
And hearts I love, and hearts that love me,
Are beating beside me merrily,

3

Yet, far in the west, where the day's faded roses,
Touched by the moonbeam, are withering fast;
Where the half-seen spirit of twilight reposes,
Hymning the dirge of the hours that are past,

4

There, where the ocean-wave sparkles at meeting
(As sunset dreams tell us) the kiss of the sky,
On his dim, dark cloud is the infant storm sitting,
And beneath the horizon his lightnings are nigh.

5

Another hour—and the death-word is given,
Another hour—and his lightnings are here;
Speed! speed thee, my bark; ere the breeze of even
Is lost in the tempest, our home will be near.

6

Then away o'er the wave, while thy pennant is streaming
In the shadowy light, like a shooting star;
Be swift as the thought of the wanderer, dreaming,
In a stranger land, of his fireside afar.

7

And while memory lingers I'll fondly believe thee
A being with life and its best feelings warm;
And freely the wild song of gratitude weave thee,
Blessed spirit! that bore me and mine from the storm.

CIV.

But where is Fanny? She has long been thrown
  Where cheeks and roses wither—in the shade.
The age of chivalry, you know, is gone;
  And although, as I once before have said,
I love a pretty face to adoration,
Yet, still, I must preserve my reputation,

CV.

As a true dandy of the modern schools.
  One hates to be oldfashioned; it would be
A violation of the latest rules,
  To treat the sex with too much courtesy.
'Tis not to worship beauty, as she glows
In all her diamond lustre, that the beaux

CVI.

Of these enlightened days at evening crowd,
  Where fashion welcomes in her rooms of light.
That "dignified obedience; that proud
  Submission," which, in times of yore, the knight
Gave to his "ladye-love," is now a scandal,
And practised only by your Goth or Vandal.

CVII.

To lounge in graceful attitudes—be stared
  Upon, the while, by every fair one's eye,
And stare one's self, in turn: to be prepared
  To dart upon the trays, as swiftly by
The dexterous Simon bears them, and to take
One's share, at least, of coffee, cream, and cake,

CVIII.

Is now to be "the ton." The pouting lip,
  And sad, upbraiding eye of the poor girl,
Who hardly of joy's cup one drop can sip,
  Ere in the wild confusion, and the whirl,
And tumult of the hour, its bubbles vanish,
Must now be disregarded. One must banish

CIX.

Those antiquated feelings, that belong
  To feudal manners and a barbarous age.
Time was—when woman "poured her soul" in song,
  That all was hushed around. 'Tis now "the rage"
To deem a song, like bugle-tones in battle,
A signal-note, that bids each tongue's artillery rattle.

CX.

And, therefore, I have made Miss Fanny wait
  My leisure. She had changed, as you will see, as
Much as her worthy sire, and made as great
  Proficiency in taste and high ideas.
The careless smile of other days was gone,
And every gesture spoke "*q'en dira-t' on?*"

CXI.

She long had known that in her father's coffers,
  And also to his credit in the banks,
There was some cash; and therefore all the offers
  Made her, by gentlemen of the middle ranks,
Of heart and hand, had spurned, as far beneath
One whose high destiny it was to breathe,

CXII.

Ere long, the air of Broadway or Park Place,
  And reign a fairy queen in fairy land;
Display in the gay dance her form of grace,
  Or touch with rounded arm and gloveless hand,
Harp or piano.—Madame Catilani
Forgot a while, and every eye on Fanny.

CXIII.

And in anticipation of that hour,
  Her star of hope—her paradise of thought,
She'd had as many masters as the power
  Of riches could bestow; and had been taught
The thousand nameless graces that adorn
The daughters of the wealthy and high-born.

CXIV.

She had been noticed at some public places
  (The Battery, and the balls of Mr. Whale),
For hers was one of those attractive faces,
  That when you gaze upon them, never fail
To bid you look again; there was a beam,
A lustre in her eye, that oft would seem

CXV.

A little like effrontery; and yet
  The lady meant no harm; her only aim
Was but to be admired by all she met,
  And the free homage of the heart to claim;
And if she showed too plainly this intention,
Others have done the same—'twas not of her invention.

CXVI.

She shone at every concert; where are bought
  Tickets, by all who wish them, for a dollar;
She patronised the Theatre, and thought
  That Wallack looked extremely well in Rolla;
She fell in love, as all the ladies do,
With Mr. Simpson—talked as loudly, too,

CXVII.

As any beauty of the highest grade,
  To the gay circle in the box beside her;
And when the pit—half vexed and half afraid,
  With looks of smothered indignation eyed her,
She calmly met their gaze, and stood before 'em,
Smiling at vulgar taste and mock decorum.

CXVIII.

And though by no means a *bas bleu*, she had
For literature a most becoming passion;
Had skimmed the latest novels, good and bad,
And read the Croakers, when they were in fashion;
And Doctor Chalmers' sermons, of a Sunday;
And Woodworth's Cabinet, and the new Salmagundi.

CXIX.

She was among the first and warmest patrons
Of Griscom's *conversaziónes*, where
In rainbow groups, our bright-eyed maids and matrons,
On science bent, assemble; to prepare
Themselves for acting well, in life, their part
As wives and mothers. There she learned by heart

CXX.

Words, to the witches in Macbeth unknown.
  Hydraulics, *hydrostatics*, and *pneumatics*,
Dioptrics, *optics*, *katoptrics*, *carbon*,
  Chlorine, and *iodine*, and *aërostatics;*
Also,—why frogs, for want of air, expire;
And how to set the Tappan sea on fire!

CXXI.

In all the modern languages she was
  Exceedingly well versed; and had devoted,
To their attainment, far more time than has,
  By the best teachers lately, been allotted;
For she had taken lessons, twice a week,
For a full month in each; and she could speak

CXXII.

French and Italian, equally as well
  As Chinese, Portuguese, or German; and,
What is still more surprising, she could spell
  Most of our longest English words off-hand;
Was quite familiar in Low Dutch and Spanish,
And thought of studying modern Greek and Danish.

CXXIII.

She sang divinely: and in "Love's young dream,"
  And "Fanny dearest," and "The soldier's bride;"
And every song, whose dear delightful theme,
  Is "Love, still love," had oft till midnight tried
Her finest, loftiest "pigeon-wings" of sound,
Waking the very watchmen far around.

CXXIV.

For her pure taste in dress, I can appeal to
  Madame Bouquet, and Monsieur Pardessus;
She was, in short, a woman you might kneel to,
  If kneeling were in fashion; or if you
Were wearied of your duns and single life,
And wanted a few thousands and a wife.

CXXV.

* * * * * * * * * * * * *
* * * * * * * * * * * * *

CXXVI.

"There was a sound of revelry by night;"
Broadway was thronged with coaches, and within
A mansion of the best of brick, the bright
And eloquent eyes of beauty bade begin
The dance; and music's tones swelled wild and high,
And hearts and heels kept tune in tremulous ecstasy.

CXXVII.

For many a week, the note of preparation
Had sounded through all circles far and near;
And some five hundred cards of invitation
Bade beau and belle in full costume appear;
There was a most magnificent variety,
All quite select, and of the first society.

CXXVIII.

That is to say—the rich and the well-bred,
The arbiters of fashion and gentility,
In different grades of splendor, from the head
Down to the very toe of our nobility:
Ladies, remarkable for handsome eyes
Or handsome fortunes—learned men, and wise

CXXIX.

Statesmen, and officers of the militia—
In short, the "first society"—a phrase,
Which you may understand as best may fit you;
Besides the blackest fiddlers of those days,
Placed like their sire, Timotheus, on high,
With horsehair fiddle-bows and teeth of ivory.

CXXX.

The carpets were rolled up the day before,
  And, with a breath, two rooms became but one,
Like man and wife—and, on the polished floor,
  Chalk in the artists' plastic hand had done
All that chalk could do—in young Eden's bowers
They seemed to tread, and their feet pressed on flowers.

CXXXI.

And when the thousand lights of spermaceti
  Streamed like a shower of sunbeams—and free tresses
Wild as the heads that waved them—and a pretty
  Collection of the latest Paris dresses
Wandered about the rooms like things divine,
It was, as I was told, extremely fine.

CXXXII.

The love of fun, fine faces, and good eating,
Brought many who were tired of self and home;
And some were there in the high hope of meeting
The lady of their bosom's love—and some
To study that deep science, how to please,
And manners in high life, and high-souled courtesies.

CXXXIII.

And he, the hero of the night, was there,
In breeches of light drab, and coat of blue.
Taste was conspicuous in his powdered hair,
And in his frequent *jeux de mots*, that drew
Peals of applauses from the listeners round,
Who were delighted—as in duty bound.

CXXXIV.

'Twas Fanny's father—Fanny near him stood,
  Her power, resistless—and her wish, command;
And Hope's young promises were all made good;
  "She reigned a fairy queen in fairy land;"
Her dream of infancy a dream no more,
And then how beautiful the dress she wore!

CXXXV.

Ambition with the sire had kept her word.
  He had the rose, no matter for its thorn,
And he seemed happy as a summer bird,
  Careering on wet wing to meet the morn.
Some said there was a cloud upon his brow;
It might be—but we'll not discuss that now.

CXXXVI.

I left him making rhymes while crossing o'er
The broad and perilous wave of the North River.
He bade adieu, when safely on the shore,
To poetry—and, as he thought, for ever.
That night his dream (if after deeds make known
Our plans in sleep) was an enchanting one.

CXXXVII.

He woke, in strength, like Samson from his slumber,
And walked Broadway, enraptured the next day;
Purchased a house there—I've forgot the number—
And signed a mortgage and a bond, for pay.
Gave, in the slang phrase, Pearl-street the go-by,
And cut, for several months, St. Tammany.

CXXXVIII.

Bond, mortgage, title-deeds, and all completed,
He bought a coach and half a dozen horses
(The bill's at Lawrence's—not yet receipted—
You'll find the amount upon his list of losses),
Then filled his rooms with servants, and whatever
Is necessary for a "genteel liver."

CXXXIX.

This last removal fixed him: every stain
Was blotted from his "household coat," and he
Now "showed the world he was a gentleman,"
And, what is better, could afford to be;
His step was loftier than it was of old,
His laugh less frequent, and his manner told

CXL.

What lovers call "unutterable things"—
That sort of dignity was in his mien
Which awes the gazer into ice, and brings
To recollection some great man we've seen,
The Governor, perchance, whose eye and frown,
'Twas shrewdly guessed, would knock Judge Skinner down.

CXLI.

And for "Resources," both of purse and head,
He was a subject worthy Bristed's pen;
Believed devoutly all his flatterers said,
And deemed himself a Crœsus among men;
Spread to the liberal air his silken sails,
And lavished guineas like a Prince of Wales.

CXLII.

He mingled now with those within whose veins
The blood ran pure—the magnates of the land—
Hailed them as his companions and his friends,
And lent them money and his note of hand.
In every institution, whose proud aim
Is public good alone, he soon became

CXLIII.

A man of consequence and notoriety;
His name, with the addition of esquire,
Stood high upon the list of each society,
Whose zeal and watchfulness the sacred fire
Of science, agriculture, art, and learning,
Keep on our country's altars bright and burning.

CXLIV.

At Eastburn's Rooms he met, at two each day,
  With men of taste and judgment like his own,
And played "first fiddle" in that orchestra
  Of literary worthies—and the tone
Of his mind's music, by the listeners caught,
Is traced among them still in language and in thought.

CXLV.

He once made the Lyceum a choice present
  Of muscle shells picked up at Rockaway;
And Mitchill gave a classical and pleasant
  Discourse about them in the streets that day,
Naming the shells, and hard to put in verse 'twas,
"Testaceous coverings of bivalve moluscas."

CXLVI.

He was a trustee of a Savings Bank,
  And lectured soundly every evil doer,
Gave dinners daily to wealth, power, and rank,
  And sixpence every Sunday to the poor;
He was a wit, in the pun-making line—
Past fifty years of age, and five feet nine.

CXLVII.

But as he trod to grandeur's pinnacle,
  With eagle eye and step that never faltered,
The busy tongue of scandal dared to tell
  That cash was scarce with him, and credit altered;
And while he stood the envy of beholders,
The Bank Directors grinned, and shrugged their shoulders.

CXLVIII.

And when these, the Lord Burleighs of the minute,
  Shake their sage heads, and look demure and holy,
Depend upon it there is something in it;
  For whether born of wisdom or of folly,
Suspicion is a being whose fell power
Blights every thing it touches, fruit and flower.

CXLIX.

Some friends (they were his creditors) once hinted
  About retrenchment and a day of doom;
He thanked them, as no doubt they kindly meant it,
  And made this speech, when they had left the room:
"Of all the curses upon mortals sent,
One's creditors are the most impudent;

CL.

"Now I am one who knows what he is doing,
And suits exactly to his means his ends;
How can a man be in the path to ruin,
When all the brokers are his bosom friends?
Yet, on my hopes, and those of my dear daughter,
These rascals throw a bucket of cold water!

CLI.

"They'd wrinkle with deep cares the prettiest face,
Pour gall and wormwood in the sweetest cup,
Poison the very wells of life—and place
Whitechapel needles, with their sharp points up,
Even in the softest feather bed that e'er
Was manufactured by upholsterer."

CLII.

This said—he journeyed "at his own sweet will,"
Like one of Wordsworth's rivers, calmly on;
But yet, at times, Reflection, "in her still
Small voice," would whisper, something must be done;
He asked advice of Fanny, and the maid
Promptly and duteously lent her aid.

CLIII.

She told him, with that readiness of mind
And quickness of perception which belong
Exclusively to gentle womankind,
That to submit to slanderers was wrong,
And the best plan to silence and admonish them,
Would be to give "a party"—and astonish them.

CLIV.

The hint was taken—and the party given;
  And Fanny, as I said some pages since,
Was there in power and loveliness that even,
  And he, her sire, demeaned him like a prince,
And all was joy—it looked a festival,
Where pain might smooth his brow, and grief her smiles
    recall.

CLV.

But Fortune, like some others of her sex,
  Delights in tantalizing and tormenting;
One day we feed upon their smiles—the next
  Is spent in swearing, sorrowing, and repenting.
(If in the last four lines the author lies,
He's always ready to apologize.)

CLVI.

Eve never walked in Paradise more pure
  Than on that morn when Satan played the devil
With her and all her race. A love-sick wooer
  Ne'er asked a kinder maiden, or more civil,
Than Cleopatra was to Antony
The day she left him on the Ionian sea.

CLVII.

The serpent—loveliest in his coiled ring,
  With eye that charms, and beauty that outvies
The tints of the rainbow—bears upon his sting
  The deadliest venom. Ere the dolphin dies
Its hues are brightest. Like an infant's breath
Are tropic winds, before the voice of death

CLVIII.

Is heard upon the waters, summoning
  The midnight earthquake from its sleep of years
To do its task of wo. The clouds that fling
  The lightning, brighten ere the bolt appears;
The pantings of the warrior's heart are proud
Upon that battle morn whose night-dews wet his shroud;

CLIX.

The sun is loveliest as he sinks to rest;
  The leaves of autumn smile when fading fast;
The swan's last song is sweetest—and the best
  Of Meigs's speeches, doubtless, was his last.
And thus the happiest scene, in these my rhymes,
Closed with a crash, and ushered in—hard times.

CLX.

St. Paul's tolled one—and fifteen minutes after
  Down came, by accident, a chandelier;
The mansion tottered from the floor to rafter!
  Up rose the cry of agony and fear!
And there was shrieking, screaming, bustling, fluttering,
Beyond the power of writing or of uttering.

CLXI.

The company departed, and neglected
  To say good-by—the father stormed and swore—
The fiddlers grinned—the daughter looked dejected—
  The flowers had vanished from the polished floor,
And both betook them to their sleepless beds,
With hearts and prospects broken, but no heads.

CLXII.

The desolate relief of free complaining
  Came with the morn, and with it came bad weather;
The wind was east-northeast, and it was raining
  Throughout that day, which, take it altogether,
Was one whose memory clings to us through life,
Just like a suit in Chancery, or a wife.

CLXIII.

That evening, with a most important face
  And dreadful knock, and tidings still more dreadful,
A notary came—sad things had taken place;
  My hero had forgot to "do the needful;"
A note (amount not stated), with his name on't,
Was left unpaid—in short, he had "stopped payment."

CLXIV.

I hate your tragedies, both long and short ones
(Except Tom Thumb, and Juan's Pantomime);
And stories woven of sorrows and misfortunes
Are bad enough in prose, and worse in rhyme;
Mine, therefore, must be brief. Under protest
His notes remain—the wise can guess the rest.

CLXV.

* * * * * * * * * * * * *
* * * * * * * * * * * * *

CLXVI.

For two whole days they were the common talk;
  The party, and the failure, and all that,
The theme of loungers in their morning walk,
  Porter-house reasoning, and tea-table chat.
The third, some newer wonder came to blot them,
And on the fourth, the "meddling world" forget them.

CLXVII.

Anxious, however, something to discover,
  I passed their house—the shutters were all closed;
The song of knocker and of bell was over;
  Upon the steps two chimney sweeps reposed;
And on the door my dazzled eyebeam met
These cabalistic words—"this house to let."

F. W. Edmonds, pinxt. Charles Burt, sculp.

And on the door my dazzled eyebeam met,
These cabalistic words — "this house to let".

Fanny.

D. Appleton & Co. New York.

CLXVIII.

They live now, like chameleons, upon air
  And hope, and such cold, unsubstantial dishes;
That they removed, is clear, but when or where
  None knew. The curious reader, if he wishes,
May ask them, but in vain. Where grandeur dwells,
The marble dome—the popular rumor tells;

CLXIX.

But of the dwelling of the proud and poor,
  From their own lips the world will never know
When better days are gone—it is secure
  Beyond all other mysteries here below,
Except, perhaps, a maiden lady's age,
When past the noonday of life's pilgrimage.

CLXX.

Fanny! 'twas with her name my song began;
'Tis proper and polite her name should end it;
If in my story of her woes, or plan
Or moral can be traced, 'twas not intended;
And if I've wronged her, I can only tell her
I'm sorry for it—so is my bookseller.

CLXXI.

I met her yesterday—her eyes were wet—
She faintly smiled, and said she had been reading
The Treasurer's Report in the Gazette,
McIntyre's speech, and Campbell's "Love lies bleeding;"
She had a shawl on, 'twas not a Cashmere one,
And if it cost five dollars, 'twas a dear one.

CLXXII.

Her father sent to Albany a prayer
For office, told how fortune had abused him,
And modestly requested to be Mayor—
The Council very civilly refused him;
Because, however much they might desire it,
The "public good," it seems, did not require it.

CLXXIII.

Some evenings since, he took a lonely stroll
Along Broadway, scene of past joys and evils;
He felt that withering bitterness of soul,
Quaintly denominated the "blue devils;"
And thought of Bonaparte and Belisarius,
Pompey, and Colonel Burr, and Caius Marius,

CLXXIV.

And envying the loud playfulness and mirth
  Of those who passed him, gay in youth and hope,
He took at Jupiter a shilling's worth
  Of gazing, through the showman's telescope;
Sounds as of far-off bells came on his ears,
He fancied 'twas the music of the spheres.

CLXXV.

He was mistaken, it was no such thing,
  'Twas Yankee Doodle played by Scudder's band;
He muttered, as he lingered listening,
  Something of freedom and our happy land;
Then sketched, as to his home he hurried fast,
This sentimental song—his saddest, and his last.

SONG.

I.

Young thoughts have music in them, love
And happiness their theme;
And music wanders in the wind
That lulls a morning dream.
And there are angel voices heard,
In childhood's frolic hours,
When life is but an April day
Of sunshine and of showers.

II.

There's music in the forest leaves
  When summer winds are there,
And in the laugh of forest girls
  That braid their sunny hair.
The first wild bird that drinks the dew,
  From violets of the spring,
Has music in his song, and in
  The fluttering of his wing.

III.

There's music in the dash of waves
  When the swift bark cleaves their foam;
There's music heard upon her deck,
  The mariner's song of home,
When moon and star beams smiling meet
  At midnight on the sea—
And there is music—once a week
  In Scudder's balcony.

IV.

But the music of young thoughts too soon
  Is faint, and dies away,
And from our morning dreams we wake
  To curse the coming day.
And childhood's frolic hours are brief,
  And oft in after years
Their memory comes to chill the heart,
  And dim the eye with tears.

V.

To-day, the forest leaves are green,
  They'll wither on the morrow,
And the maiden's laugh be changed ere long
  To the widow's wail of sorrow.
Come with the winter snows, and ask
  Where are the forest birds?
The answer is a silent one,
  More eloquent than words.

VI.

The moonlight music of the waves
  In storms is heard no more,
When the living lightning mocks the wreck
  At midnight on the shore,
And the mariner's song of home has ceased,
  His corse is on the sea—
And music ceases when it rains
  In Scudder's balcony.

THE RECORDER

THE RECORDER.

A PETITION.

BY THOMAS CASTALY.

Dec. 20, 1828.

"On they move
In perfect phalanx to the Dorian mood
Of flutes and soft RECORDERS."

MILTON.

"Live in Settles numbers one day more !"

POPE.

MY dear RECORDER, you and I
  Have floated down life's stream together,
And kept unharmed our friendship's tie
Through every change of Fortune's sky,
  Her pleasant and her rainy weather.
Full sixty times since first we met,
Our birthday suns have risen and set,

And time has worn the baldness now
Of Julius Cæsar on your brow;
Your brow, like his, a field of thought,
With broad deep furrows, spirit-wrought,
Whose laurel harvests long have shown
As green and glorious as his own;
And proudly would the Cæsar claim
Companionship with R*k*r's name,
His peer in forehead and in fame.

Both eloquent and learned and brave,
  Born to command and skilled to rule,
One made the citizen a slave,
  The other makes him more—a fool.
The Cæsar an imperial crown,
  His slaves' mad gift, refused to wear,
The R*k*r put his fool's cap on,
  And found it fitted to a hair;

The Cæsar, though by birth and breeding,
Travel, the ladies, and light reading,
  A gentleman in mien and mind,
And fond of Romans and their mothers,
Was heartless as the Arab's wind,
And slew some millions of mankind,
  Including enemies and others.
The R*k*r, like Bob Acres, stood
Edgewise upon a field of blood,
  The where and wherefore Swartwout knows,
Pulled trigger, as a brave man should,
  And shot, God bless them—his own toes.
The Cæsar passed the Rubicon
With helm, and shield, and breastplate on,
  Dashing his war-horse through the waters;
The R*k*r would have built a barge
Or steamboat at the city's charge,
  And passed it with his wife and daughters.

But let that pass. As I have said,
There's naught, save laurels, on your head,
And time has changed my clustering hair,
And showered the snow-flakes thickly there;
And though our lives have ever been,
As different as their different scene;
Mine more renowned for rhymes than riches,
Yours less for scholarship than speeches;
Mine passed in low-roofed leafy bower,
Yours in high halls of pomp and power,
Yet are we, be the moral told,
Alike in one thing—growing old,
Ripened like summer's cradled sheaf,
Faded like autumn's falling leaf—
And nearing, sail and signal spread,
The quiet anchorage of the dead.
For such is human life, wherever
 The voyage of its bark may be,

On home's green-banked and gentle river
  Or the world's shoreless, sleepless sea.

Yes, you have floated down the tide
Of time, a swan in grace and pride
And majesty and beauty, till
The law, the Ariel of your will,
Power's best beloved, the law of libel
(A bright link in the legal chain)
Expounded, settled, and made plain,
By your own charge, the jurors' Bible,
Has clipped the venomed tongue of slander,
That dared to call you "Party's gander,
The leader of the geese who make
  Our city's parks and ponds their home,
And keep her liberties awake
  By cackling, as their sires saved Rome

Gander of Party's pond, wherein
Lizard, and toad, and terrapin,
Your alehouse patriots, are seen,
  In Faction's feverish sunshine basking;"
And now, to rend this veil of lies,
Word-woven by your enemies,
And keep your sainted memory free
From tarnish with posterity,
  I take the liberty of asking
Permission, sir, to write your life,
With all its scenes of calm and strife,
  And all its turnings and its windings,
A poem, in a quarto volume—
Verse, like the subject, blank and solemn,
  With elegant appropriate bindings,
Of rat and mole skin the one half,
The other a part fox, part calf.
Your portrait, graven line for line,
From that immortal bust in plaster,
The master-piece of Art's great master,

Mr. Praxiteles Browere,
Whose trowel is a thing divine,
Shall smile and bow, and promise there,
And twenty-nine fine forms and faces
(The Corporation and the Mayor),
Linked hand in hand, like loves and graces,
Shall hover o'er it, grouped in air,
With wild pictorial dance and song;
The song of happy bees in bowers,
The dance of Guido's graceful hours,
All scattering Flushing's garden flowers
Round the dear head they've loved so long.

I know that you are modest, know
That when you hear your merit's praise,
Your cheeks' quick blushes come and go,
Lily and rose-leaf, sun and snow,
Like maidens' on their bridal days.

I know that you would fain decline
To aid me and the sacred nine,
In giving to the asking earth
The story of your wit and worth;
For if there be a fault to cloud
  The brightness of your clear good sense,
It is, and be the fact allowed,
  Your only failing—DIFFIDENCE!
An amiable weakness—given
  To justify the sad reflection,
That in this vale of tears not even
  A R*k*r is complete perfection,
A most romantic detestation
Of power and place, of pay and ration;
A strange unwillingness to carry
  The weight of honor on your shoulders,
For which you have been named, the very
  Sensitive plant of office-holders,
A shrinking bashfulness, whose grace
  Gives beauty to your manly face.

Thus shades the green and growing vine
The rough bark of the mountain pine,
Thus round her freedom's waking steel
  Harmodius wreathed his country's myrtle;
And thus the golden lemon's peel
  Gives fragrance to a bowl of turtle.

True, "many a flower," the poet sings,
  "Is born to blush unseen;"
But you, although you blush, are not
  The flower the poets mean.
In vain you wooed a lowlier lot:
  In vain you clipped your eagle-wings—
Talents like yours are not forgot
  And buried with earth's common things.
No! my dear R*k*r, I would give
My laurels, living and to live,
Or as much cash as you could raise on
Their value, by hypothecation,

To be, for one enchanted hour,
In beauty, majesty, and power,
What you for forty years have been,
The Oberon of life's fairy scene.

An anxious city sought and found you
  In a blessed day of joy and pride,
Sceptred your jewelled hand, and crowned you
  Her chief, her guardian, and her guide.
Honors which weaker minds had wrought
  In vain for years, and knelt and prayed for,
Are all your own, unpriced, unbought,
  Or (which is the same thing) unpaid for.
Painfully great! against your will
  Her hundred offices to hold,
Each chair with dignity to fill,
  And your own pockets with her gold:
A sort of double duty, making
Your task a serious undertaking.

With what delight the eyes of all
Gaze on you, seated in your Hall,
  Like Sancho in his island, reigning,
Loved leader of its motley hosts
Of lawyers and their bills of costs,
  And all things thereto appertaining,
Such as crimes, constables, and juries,
Male pilferers and female furies,
The police and the *polissons*,
Illegal right and legal wrong,
Bribes, perjuries, law-craft, and cunning,
Judicial drollery and punning;
And all the *et ceteras* that grace
That genteel, gentlemanly place!
Or in the Council Chamber standing
  With eloquence of eye and brow,
Your voice the music of commanding,
  And fascination in your bow,

Arranging for the civic shows
  Your "men in buckram," as per list,
Your John Does and your Richard Roes,
  Those Dummys of your games of whist.
The Council Chamber—where authority
Consists in two words—a majority.
For whose contractors' jobs we pay
  Our last dear sixpences for taxes,
As freely as in Sylla's day,
  Rome bled beneath his lictors' axes.
Where—on each magisterial nose
  In colors of the rainbow linger,
Like sunset hues on Alpine snows,
  The printmarks of your thumb and finger
Where he, the wisest of wild fowl,
Bird of Jove's blue-eyed maid—the owl,
  That feathered alderman, is heard
Nightly, by poet's ear alone,
To other eyes and ears unknown,
  Cheering your every look and word,

And making, room and gallery through,
  The loud, applauding echoes peal,
Of his "*où peut on être mieux*
Qu'au sein de sa famille?"*

Oh for a herald's skill to rank
  Your titles in their due degrees!
At Singsing—at the Tradesmen's Bank,
  In Courts, Committees, Caucuses:
At Albany, where those who knew
  The last year's secrets of the great,
Call you the golden handle to
  The earthen Pitcher of the State.
(Poor Pitcher! that Van Buren ceases
  To want its service gives me pain,
'Twill break into as many pieces

* A favorite French air. In English, "where can one be more happy than in tho bosom of one's family?"

As Kitty's of Coleraine.)
At Bellevue, on her banquet night,
Where Burgundy and business meet,
On others, at the heart's delight,
The Pewter Mug in Frankfort-street;
From Harlæm bridge to Whitehall dock,
From Bloomingdale to Blackwell's Isles,
Forming, including road and rock,
A city of some twelve square miles,
O'er street and alley, square and block,
Towers, temples, telegraphs, and tiles,
O'er wharves whose stone and timbers mock
The ocean's and its navies' shock,
O'er all the fleets that float before her,
O'er all their banners waving o'er her,
Her sky and waters, earth and air—
You are lord, for who is her lord mayor?
Where is he? Echo answers, where?
And voices, like the sound of seas,
Breathe in sad chorus, on the breeze,

The Highland mourner's melody—
Oh Hone a rie! Oh Hone a rie!
The hymn o'er happy days departed,
  The hope that such again may be,
When power was large and liberal-hearted,
  And wealth was hospitality.

One more request, and I am lost,
  If you its earnest prayer deny;
It is, that you preserve the most
  Inviolable secrecy
As to my plan. Our fourteen wards
Contain some thirty-seven bards,
Who, if my glorious theme were known,
Would make it, thought and word, their own,
My hopes and happiness destroy,
And trample with a rival's joy
  Upon the grave of my renown.

My younger brothers in the art,
Whose study is the human heart—
Minstrels, before whose spells have bowed
The learned, the lovely, and the proud,
  Ere their life's morning hours are gone—
Light hearts be theirs, the muse's boon,
And may their suns blaze bright at noon,
  And set without a cloud.

Hillhouse, whose music, like his themes,
Lifts earth to heaven—whose poet dreams
Are pure and holy as the hymn
Echoed from harps of seraphim,
By bards that drank at Zion's fountains
  When glory, peace, and hope were hers,
And beautiful upon her mountains
  The feet of angel messengers.

BRYANT, whose songs are thoughts that bless
  The heart, its teachers, and its joy,
As mothers blend with their caress
Lessons of truth and gentleness
  And virtue for the listening boy.
Spring's lovelier flowers for many a day
Have blossomed on his wandering way,
Beings of beauty and decay,
  They slumber in their autumn tomb;
But those that graced his own Green River,
  And wreathed the lattice of his home,
Charmed by his song from mortal doom,
  Bloom on, and will bloom on for ever.
And HALLECK—who has made thy roof,
St. Tammany! oblivion-proof—
Thy beer illustrious, and thee
A belted knight of chivalry;
And changed thy dome of painted bricks
And porter casks and politics,
  Into a green Arcadian vale,

With St*ph*n All*n for its lark,
B*n B*il*y's voice its watch-dog's bark,
  And J*hn T*rg*e its nightingale.

These, and the other THIRTY-FOUR,
Will live a thousand years or more—
If the world lasts so long. For me,
I rhyme not for posterity,
Though pleasant to my heirs might be
  The incense of its praise,
When I their ancestor, have gone,
And paid the debt, the only one
  A poet ever pays.
But many are my years, and few
Are left me ere night's holy dew,
And sorrow's holier tears, will keep
The grass green where in death I sleep.
And when that grass is green above me,
And those who bless me now and love me

Are sleeping by my side,
Will it avail me aught that men
Tell to the world with lip and pen
That once I lived and died?
No: if a garland for my brow
Is growing, let me have it now,
While I'm alive to wear it;
And if, in whispering my name,
There's music in the voice of fame
Like Garcia's, let me hear it!

The Christmas holydays are nigh,
Therefore, till Newyear's Eve, good-by,
Then "*revenons a nos moutons*,"
Yourself and aldermen—meanwhile,
Look o'er this letter with a smile;
And keep the secret of its song
As faithfully, but not as long,

As you have guarded from the eyes
Of editorial Paul Prys,
  And other meddling, murmuring claimants,
Those Eleusinian mysteries,
  The city's cash receipts and payments.

Yours ever,

T. C.

EPISTLES, ETC.

TO W*LT*R B*WNE, ESQ.,

MEMBER OF THE COUNCIL OF APPOINTMENT OF THE STATE OF NEW-YORK, AT ALBANY, 1821.

"Stand not upon the order of your going,
But go at once."

"I cannot but remember such things were,
And were most precious to me."

MACBETH.

We do not blame you, W*lt*r B*wne,
For a variety of reasons;
You're now the talk of half the town,
A man of talent and renown,
And will be for perhaps two seasons.

That face of yours has magic in it;
Its smile transports us in a minute
To wealth and pleasure's sunny bowers;
And there is terror in its frown,
Which, like a mower's scythe, cuts down
Our city's loveliest flowers.

We therefore do not blame you, sir,
Whate'er our cause of grief may be;
And cause enough we have to "stir
The very stones to mutiny."
You've driven from the cash and cares
Of office, heedless of our prayers,
Men who have been for many a year
To us and to our purses dear,
And will be to our heirs for ever,
Our tears, thanks to the snow and rain,
Have swelled the brook in Maiden-lane
Into a mountain river;

And when you visit us again,
Leaning at Tammany on your cane,
Like warrior on his battle blade,
You'll mourn the havoc you have made.

There is a silence and a sadness
  Within the marble mansion now;
Some have wild eyes that threaten madness,
  Some think of "kicking up a row."
Judge M*ll*r will not yet believe
That you have ventured to bereave
  The city and its hall of him:
He has in his own fine way stated,
"The fact must be substantiated,"
  Before he'll move a single limb.
He deems it cursed hard to yield
The laurel won in every field
  Through sixteen years of party war,

And to be seen at noon no more,
Enjoying at his office door
  The luxury of a tenth segar.
Judge Warner says that, when he's gone,
  You'll miss the true Dogberry breed;
And Christian swears that you have done
  A most UN-Christian deed.

How could you have the heart to strike
From place the peerless Pierre Van Wyck?
And the twin colonels, Haines and Pell,
Squire Fessenden, and Sheriff Bell;
M*rr*ll, a justice and a wise one,
And Ned M'Laughlin the exciseman;
The two health officers, believers
In Clinton and contagious fevers;
The keeper of the city's treasures,
The sealer of her weights and measures,

The harbor-master, her best bower
Cable in party's stormy hour;
Ten auctioneers, three bank directors,
And Mott and Duffy, the inspectors
  Of whiskey and of flour?

It was but yesterday they stood
All (ex-officio) great and good.
But by the tomahawk struck down
Of party and of W*lt*r B*wne,
Where are they now? With shapes of air,
The caravan of things that were,
Journeying to their nameless home,
Like Mecca's pilgrims from her tomb;
With the lost Pleiad; with the wars
Of Agamemnon's ancestors;
With their own years of joy and grief,
Spring's bud, and autumn's faded leaf;

With birds that round their cradles flew;
With winds that in their boyhood blew;
With last night's dream and last night's dew.

Yes, they are gone; alas! each one of them;
Departed—every mother's son of them.
Yet often, at the close of day,
When thoughts are winged and wandering, they
Come with the memory of the past,
  Like sunset clouds along the mind,
Reflecting, as they're flitting fast
In their wild hues of shade and light,
All that was beautiful and bright
  In golden moments left behind.

TO *****.

Dear ***, I am writing, not *to* you, but *at* you,
For the feet of you tourists have no resting-place;
But wherever with this the mail-pigeon may catch you,
May she find you with gayety's smile on your face;
Whether chasing a snipe at the Falls of Cohoes,
Or chased by the snakes upon Anthony's Nose;
Whether wandering, at Catskill, from Hotel to Clove,
Making sketches, or speeches, puns, poems, or love;
Or in old Saratoga's unknown fountain-land,
Threading groves of enchantment, half bushes, half sand:

Whether dancing on Sundays, at Lebanon Springs,
  With those Madame Hutins of religion, the Shakers;
Or, on Tuesdays, with maidens who seek wedding-rings
  At Ballston, as taught by mammas and match-makers;
Whether sailing St. Lawrence, with unbroken neck,
From her thousand green isles to her castled Quebec;
Or sketching Niagara, pencil on knee
  (The giant of waters, our country's pet lion),
Or dipped at Long Branch, in the real salt sea,
  With a cork for a dolphin, a Cockney Arion;
Whether roaming earth, ocean, or even the air,
Like Dan O'Rourke's eagle—good luck to you there.

For myself, as you'll see by the date of my letter,
I'm in town, but of that fact the least said the better;
For 'tis vain to deny (though the city o'erflows
With well-dressed men and women, whom nobody knows)
That one rarely sees persons whose nod is an honor,
A lady with fashion's own impress upon her;

Or a gentleman blessed with the courage to say,
Like Morris (the Prince Regent's friend, in his day),
"Let others in sweet shady solitudes dwell,
Oh! give me the sweet shady side of Pall Mall."

Apropos—our friend A. chanced this morning to meet
The accomplished Miss B. as he passed Contoit's Garden,
Both in town in July!—he crossed over the street,
And she entered the rouge-shop of Mrs. St. Martin.
Resolved not to look at another known face,
Through Leonard and Church streets she walked to Park Place,
And he turned from Broadway into Catharine-lane,
And coursed, to avoid her, through alley and by-street,
Till they met, as the devil would have it, again,
Face to face, near the pump at the corner of Dey-street.

Yet, as most of "The Fashion" are journeying now,
With the brown hues of summer on cheek and on brow,
The few "*gens comme il faut*" who are lingering here,
Are, like fruits out of season, more welcome and dear.
Like "the last rose of summer, left blooming alone,"
Or the last snows of winter, pure ice of *haut ton*,
Unmelted, undimmed by the sun's brightest ray,
And, like diamonds, making night's darkness seem day.
One meets them in groups, that Canova might fancy,
At our new lounge at evening, the *Opera Français*,
In nines like the Muses, in threes like the Graces,
Green spots in a desert of commonplace faces.
The Queen, Mrs. Adams, goes there sweetly dressed
  In a beautiful bonnet, all golden and flowery:
While the King, Mr. Bonaparte, smiles on Celeste,
  Heloise, and Hutin, from his box at the Bowery.

For news, Parry still the North Sea is exploring,
And the Grand Turk has taken, they say, the Acropolis,
And we, in Swamp Place, have discovered, in boring,
A mineral spring to refine the metropolis.
The day we discovered it was, by-the-way
In the life of the Cockneys, a glorious day.
For we all had been taught, by tradition and reading,
That to gain what admits us to levees of kings,
The gentleness, courtesy, grace of high breeding,
The only sure way was to "visit the Springs."
So the whole city visited Swamp Spring *en masse*,
From attorney to sweep, from physician to pavior,
To drink of cold water at sixpence a glass,
And learn true politeness and genteel behavior.
Though the crowd was immense till the hour of departure,
No gentleman's feelings were hurt in the rush,
Save a grocer's, who lost his proof-glass and bung-starter,
And a chimney-sweep's, robbed of his scraper and brush.

They lingered till sunset and twilight had come,
  Then, wearied in limb, but much polished in manners,
The sovereign people moved gracefully home,
  In the beauty and pride of "an army with banners."

As to politics—Adams and Clinton yet live,
  And reign, we presume, as we never have missed 'em,
And woollens and Webster continue to thrive
  Under something they call the American System.
If you're anxious to know what the country is doing,
Whether ruined already or going to ruin,
  And who her next president will be, please heaven,
Read the letters of Jackson, the speeches of Clay,
All the party newspapers, three columns a day,
  And Blunt's Annual Register, year 'twenty-seven.

* * *

A FRAGMENT.

---

* * * * * * * *

His shop is a grocer's—a snug, genteel place,
  Near the corner of Oak-street and Pearl;
He can dress, dance, and bow to the ladies with grace,
  And ties his cravat with a curl.

He's asked to all parties—north, south, east, and west,
  That take place between Chatham and Cherry,
And when he's been absent full oft has the "best
  Society" ceased to be merry.

And nothing has darkened a sky so serene,
  Nor disordered his beauship's Elysium,
Till this season among our *élite* there has been
  What is called by the clergy "a schism."

'Tis all about eating and drinking—one set
  Gives sponge-cake, a few "kisses" or so,
And is cooled after dancing with classic sherbet,
  "Sublimed" (see Lord Byron) "with snow."

Another insists upon punch and *perdrix*,
  Lobster-salad, Champagne, and, by way
Of a novelty only, those pearls of our sea,
  Stewed oysters from Lynn-Haven bay.

Miss Flounce, the young milliner, blue-eyed and bright,
In the front parlor over her shop,
"Entertains," as the phrase is, a party to-night,
Upon peanuts and ginger-pop.

And Miss Fleece, who's a hosier, and not quite as young,
But is wealthier far than Miss Flounce,
She "entertains" also to-night with cold tongue,
Smoked herring, and cherry-bounce.

In praise of cold water the Theban bard spoke,
He of Teos sang sweetly of wine;
Miss Flounce is a Pindar in cashmere and cloak,
Miss Fleece an Anacreon divine.

The Montagues carry the day in Swamp Place;
In Pike-street the Capulets reign;
A *limonadière* is the badge of one race,
Of the other a flask of Champagne.

Now as each the same evening her *soirée* announces,
  What better, he asks, can be done,
Than drink water from eight until ten with the Flounces,
  And then wine with the Fleeces till one!

* * * * * * * *

SONG.

BY MISS ****.

AIR: "To ladies' eyes a round, boy."
MOORE.

THE winds of March are humming
  Their parting song, their parting song,
And summer's skies are coming,
  And days grow long, and days grow long.
I watch, but not in gladness,
  Our garden tree, our garden tree;
It buds, in sober sadness,
  Too soon for me, too soon for me.

My second winter's over,
  Alas! and I, alas! and I
Have no accepted lover:
  Don't ask me why, don't ask me why.

'Tis not asleep or idle
  That love has been, that love has been;
For many a happy bridal
  The year has seen, the year has seen;
I've done a bridemaid's duty,
  At three or four, at three or four;
My best bouquet had beauty,
  Its donor more, its donor more.
My second winter's over,
  Alas! and I, alas! and I
Have no accepted lover:
  Don't ask me why, don't ask me why.

His flowers my bosom shaded
  One sunny day, one sunny day;
The next, they fled and faded,
  Beau and bouquet, beau and bouquet.
In vain, at ball and parties,
  I've thrown my net, I've thrown my net;
This waltzing, watching heart is
  Unchosen yet, unchosen yet.
      My second winter's over,
        Alas! and I, alas! and I
      Have no accepted lover:
        Don't ask me why, don't ask me why.

They tell me there's no hurry
  For Hymen's ring, for Hymen's ring;
And I'm too young to marry:
  'Tis no such thing, 'tis no such thing.

The next spring tides will dash on
  My eighteenth year, my eighteenth year;
It puts me in a passion,
  Oh dear, oh dear! oh dear, oh dear!
    My second winter's over,
      Alas! and I, alas! and I
    Have no accepted lover:
      Don't ask me why, don't ask me why.

SONG.

FOR THE DRAMA OF "THE SPY."

THE harp of love, when first I heard
  Its song beneath the moonlight tree,
Was echoed by his plighted word,
  And ah, how dear its song to me;
But wailed the hour will ever be
  When to the air the bugle gave,
To hush love's gentle minstrelsy,
  The wild war music of the brave.

For he hath heard its song, and now
  Its voice is sweeter than mine own;
And he hath broke the plighted vow
  He breathed to me and love alone.
That harp hath lost its wonted tone,
  No more its strings his fingers move,
Oh would that he had only known
  The music of the harp of love.

1822.

ADDRESS,

AT THE OPENING OF A NEW THEATRE,

November, 1831.

WHERE dwells the Drama's spirit? not alone
Beneath the palace roof, beside the throne,
In learning's cloisters, friendship's festal bowers,
Art's pictured halls, or triumph's laurelled towers,
Where'er man's pulses beat or passions play,
She joys to smile or sigh his thoughts away:
Crowd times and scenes within her ring of power,
And teach a life's experience in an hour.

To-night she greets, for the first time, our dome,
Her latest, may it prove her lasting home;
And we her messengers delighted stand,
The summoned Ariels of her mystic wand,
To ask your welcome. Be it yours to give
Bliss to her coming hours, and bid her live
Within these walls new hallowed in her cause,
Long in the nurturing warmth of your applause.

'Tis in the public smiles, the public loves,
His dearest home, the actor breathes and moves,
Your plaudits are to us and to our art
As is the life-blood to the human heart:
And every power that bids the leaf be green,
In nature acts on this her mimic scene.
Our sunbeams are the sparklings of glad eyes,
Our winds the whisper of applause, that flies

From lip to lip, the heart-born laugh of glee,
And sounds of cordial hands that ring out merrily,
And heaven's own dew falls on us in the tear
That woman weeps o'er sorrows pictured here,
When crowded feelings have no words to tell
The might, the magic of the actor's spell.

These have been ours; and do we hope in vain
Here, oft and deep, to feel them ours again?
No! while the weary heart can find repose
From its own pains in fiction's joys or woes;
While there are open lips and dimpled cheeks,
When music breathes, or wit or humor speaks;
While Shakspeare's master spirit can call up
Noblest and worthiest thoughts, and brim the cup
Of life with bubbles bright as happiness,
Cheating the willing bosom into bliss;
So long will those who, in their spring of youth,
Have listened to the Drama's voice of truth,

Marked in her scenes the manners of their age,
And gathered knowledge for a wider stage,
Come here to speed with smiles life's summer years,
And melt its winter snow with pleasant tears;
And younger hearts, when ours are hushed and cold,
Be happy here as we have been of old.

Friends of the stage, who hail it as the shrine
Where music, painting, poetry entwine
Their kindred garlands, whence their blended power
Refines, exalts, ennobles hour by hour
The spirit of the land, and, like the wind,
Unseen but felt, bears on the bark of mind;
To you the hour that consecrates this dome,
Will call up dreams of prouder hours to come,
When some creating poet, born your own,
May waken here the drama's loftiest tone,
Through after years to echo loud and long,
A Shakspeare of the West, a star of song,

Bright'ning your own blue skies with living fire,
All times to gladden and all tongues inspire,
Far as beneath the heaven by sea-winds fanned,
Floats the free banner of your native land.

THE RHYME

OF

THE ANCIENT COASTER.

WRITTEN WHILE SAILING IN AN OPEN BOAT ON THE HUDSON RIVER, BETWEEN STONY POINT AND THE HIGHLANDS, ON SEEING THE WRECK OF AN OLD SLOOP, JUNE, 1821.

"And this our life, exempt from public haunt,
Finds tongues in trees, books in the running brooks,
Sermons in stones, and good in every thing."

SHAKSPEARE.

HER side is in the water,
Her keel is in the sand,
And her bowsprit rests on the low gray rock
That bounds the sea and land.

Her deck is without a mast,
And sand and shells are there,
And the teeth of decay are gnawing her planks,
In the sun and the sultry air.

No more on the river's bosom,
When sky and wave are calm,
And the clouds are in summer quietness,
And the cool night-breath is balm,

Will she glide in the swan-like stillness
Of the moon in the blue above,
A messenger from other lands,
A beacon to hope and love.

No more, in the midnight tempest,
Will she mock the mounting sea,
Strong in her oaken timbers,
And her white sail's bravery.

She hath borne, in days departed,
    Warm hearts upon her deck;
Those hearts, like her, are mouldering now,
    The victims, and the wreck

Of time, whose touch erases
    Each vestige of all we love;
The wanderers, home returning,
    Who gazed that deck above,

And they who stood to welcome
    Their loved ones on that shore,
Are gone, and the place that knew them
    Shall know them never more.

* * * * * * *
* * * * * * *

It was a night of terror,
In the autumn equinox,
When that gallant vessel found a grave
Upon the Peekskill rocks.

Captain, mate, cook, and seamen
(They were in all but three),
Were saved by swimming fast and well,
And their gallows-destiny.

But two, a youth and maiden,
Were left to brave the storm,
With unpronounceable Dutch names,
And hearts with true love warm.

And they, for love has watchers
In air, on earth, and sea,
Were saved by clinging to the wreck,
And their marriage-destiny.

From sunset to night's noon
    She had leaned upon his arm,
Nor heard the far-off thunder toll
    The tocsin of alarm.

Not so the youth—he listened
    To the cloud-wing flapping by;
And low he whispered in Low Dutch,
    "It tells our doom is nigh.

"Death is the lot of mortals,
    But we are young and strong,
And hoped, not boldly, for a life
    Of happy years and long.

"Yet 'tis a thought consoling,
    That, till our latest breath,
We loved in life, and shall not be
    Divided in our death.

"Alas, for those that wait us
On their couch of dreams at home,
The morn will hear the funeral cry
Around their daughter's tomb.

"They hoped" ('twas a strange moment
In Dutch to quote Shakspeare)
"Thy bride-bed to have decked, sweet maid,
And not have strewed thy bier."

But, sweetly-voiced and smiling,
The trusting maiden said,
"Breathed not thy lips the vow to-day,
To-morrow we will wed?

"And I, who have known thy truth
Through years of joy and sorrow,
Can I believe the fickle winds?
No! we shall wed to-morrow!"

The tempest heard and paused—
The wild sea gentler moved—
They felt the power of woman's faith
In the word of him she loved.

All night to rope and spar
They clung with strength untired,
Till the dark clouds fled before the sun,
And the fierce storm expired.

At noon the song of bridal bells
O'er hill and valley ran;
At eve he called the maiden his,
"Before the holy man."

They dwelt beside the waters
That bathe yon fallen pine,
And round them grew their sons and daughters,
Like wild grapes on the vine.

And years and years flew o'er them,
    Like birds with beauty on their wings,
And theirs were happy sleigh-ride winters,
    And long and lovely springs,

Such joys as thrilled the lips that kissed,
    The wave, rock-cooled, from Horeb's fountains,
And sorrows, fleeting as the mist
    Of morning, spread upon the mountains,

Till, in a good old age,
    Their life-breath passed away;
Their name is on the churchyard page—
    Their story in my lay.

* * * * * * *
* * * * * * *

And let them rest together,
    The maid, the boat, the boy,
Why sing of matrimony now,
    In this brief hour of joy?

Our time may come, and let it—
    'Tis enough for us now to know
That our bark will reach West Point ere long,
    If the breeze keep on to blow.

We have Hudibras and Milton,
    Wines, flutes, and a bugle-horn,
And a dozen segars are lingering yet
    Of the thousand of yestermorn.

They have gone, like life's first pleasures,
    And faded in smoke away,
And the few that are left are like bosom friends
    In the evening of our day.

We are from the mount of battle,*
    Where the wreck first met mine eye,
And now where twin-forts† in the olden time rose,
Through the Race, like a swift steed, our little bark goes,
And our bugle's notes echo through Anthony's Nose,
    So wrecks and rhymes—good-by.

* Stony Point. † Forts Clinton and Montgomery.

LINES

TO HER WHO CAN UNDERSTAND THEM.

AIR: "To ladies' eyes a round, boy!"

THE song that o'er me hovered,
  In summer's hour, in summer's hour,
To-day with joy has covered
  My winter bower, my winter bower.

Blest be the lips that breathe it,
  As mine have been, as mine have been,
When pressed in dreams beneath it,
  To hers unseen, to hers unseen.
And may her heart, wherever
  Its hope may be, its hope may be,
Beat happily, though never
  To beat for me, to beat for me.

Is she a spirit given
  One hour to earth, one hour to earth,
To bring me dreams from heaven,
  Her place of birth, her place of birth?
Or minstrel maiden hidden,
  Like cloistered nun, like cloistered nun,
A bud, a flower forbidden,
  To air and sun, to air and sun?

For had I power to summon,
  With harp divine, with harp divine,
The angel or the woman,
  The last were mine, the last were mine.

If earth-born beauty's fingers
  Awaked the lay, awaked the lay,
Whose echoed music lingers
  Around my way, around my way,
Where smiles the hearth she blesses
  With voice and eye, with voice and eye?
Where binds the night her tresses,
  When sleep is nigh, when sleep is nigh?
Is Fashion's bleak cold mountain
  Her bosom's throne, her bosom's throne?
Or Love's green vale and fountain,
  With one alone, with one alone?

Why ask? why seek a treasure
  Like her I sing, like her I sing?
Her name nor pain nor pleasure
  To me should bring, to me should bring.
Love must not grieve or gladden
  My thoughts of snow, my thoughts of snow,
Nor woman soothe or sadden
  My path below, my path below.
Before a worldlier altar
  I've knelt too long, I've knelt too long;
And if my footsteps falter
  'Tis but in song, 'tis but in song.

Nor would I break the vision
  Young fancies frame, young fancies frame,
That lights with stars Elysian
  A poet's name, a poet's name.

For she whose gentle spirit
  Such dreams sublime, such dreams sublime,
Gives hues they do not merit
  To sons of rhyme, to sons of rhyme.
But place the proudest near her,
  Whate'er his pen, whate'er his pen,
She'll say (be mute who hear her)
  Mere mortal men, mere mortal men!

Yet though unseen, unseeing,
  We meet and part, we meet and part,
Be still my worshipped being,
  In mind and heart, in mind and heart.
And bid thy song that found me,
  My minstrel maid, my minstrel maid!
Be wintry sunbeam round me,
  And summer's shade, and summer's shade.

I could not gaze upon thee,
  And dare thy spell, and dare thy spell,
And when a happier won thee,
  Thus bid farewell, thus bid farewell.

1832.

FINIS.

NOTES.

1) Page 11.—ALNWICK CASTLE, Northumberlandshire, a seat of the Duke of Northumberland. Written in October, 1822.

From him who once his standard set.—Page 14.

(2) One of the ancestors of the Percy family was an Emperor of Constantinople.

Fought for King George at Lexington.—Page 15.

(3) The late duke. He commanded a detachment of the British army, in the affair at Lexington and Concord, in 1775.

From royal Berwick's beach of sand.—Page 15.

(4) Berwick was formerly a principality. Richard II. was styled "King of England, France, and Ireland, and Berwick-upon-Tweed."

(5) Page 19.—MARCO BOZZARIS, one of the best and bravest of the modern Greek chieftains. He fell in a night attack upon the Turkish camp at Laspi, the site of the ancient Platæa, August 20, 1823, and expired in the moment of victory.

(6) Page 36.—Wyoming.—The allusions in the following stanzas can be understood by those only who have read Campbell's beautiful poem, "Gertrude of Wyoming:" but who has not read it?

(7) Page 60.—"Red Jacket" appeared originally in 1828, soon after the publication of Mr. Cooper's "Notions of the Americans."

(8) Page 76.—Magdalen.—Written in 1823, for a love-stricken young officer on his way to Greece. The reader will have the kindness to presume that he died there.

(9) Page 106.—Lieut. Allen.—He commanded the U. S. Sloop-of-War Alligator, and was mortally wounded on the 9th of November, 1822, in an action with pirates, near Matanzas, in the Island of Cuba. His mother, a few hours after hearing of his death, died—literally of a broken heart.

www.ingramcontent.com/pod-product-compliance
Lightning Source LLC
LaVergne TN
LVHW010217110826
845151LV00004B/1113

* 9 7 8 1 4 2 5 5 2 6 8 5 6 *